FREEDOM

FREEDOM

How We
Lose It

AND How We
Fight Back

NATHAN LAW

with Evan Fowler

THE EXPERIMENT

NEW YORK

FREEDOM: *How We Lose It and How We Fight Back*
Copyright © 2021 by Kwun Chung Law
Nathan Law has asserted his moral right to be identified as the author of
this work.

Originally published in Great Britain by Bantam Press, an imprint of Transworld
Publishers, part of the Penguin Random House group. First published in North
America in revised form by The Experiment, LLC.

The Experiment, LLC
220 East 23rd Street, Suite 600
New York, NY 10010-4658
theexperimentpublishing.com

THE EXPERIMENT and its colophon are registered trademarks of
The Experiment, LLC. Many of the designations used by manufacturers and
sellers to distinguish their products are claimed as trademarks. Where those
designations appear in this book and The Experiment was aware of a trademark
claim, the designations have been capitalized.

The Experiment's books are available at special discounts when purchased in bulk
for premiums and sales promotions as well as for fundraising or educational use.
For details, contact us at info@theexperimentpublishing.com.

Library of Congress Cataloging-in-Publication Data available upon request

ISBN 978-1-61519-890-0
Ebook ISBN 978-1-61519-891-7

Cover design by Beth Bugler
Text design by Couper Street Type Co.
Author photograph courtesy of the author

Manufactured in the United States of America

First printing December 2021
10 9 8 7 6 5 4 3 2 1

This book is dedicated to all Hongkongers who have marched in the streets to fight for our freedoms. Their sacrifices, especially those of my friends who have been imprisoned in their pursuit of democracy, should not be forgotten.

CONTENTS

PREFACE

What is freedom? And what does it mean to live in a free society? These are two of the most profound questions we can ask. They have inspired passionate debate across the globe, and across civilizations, for a very long time. In the West, the philosophical tradition of freedom is often traced to the Greeks, and to its personification in the idea of liberty or *eleutheria*. In China, questions of freedom were also central to the writings of Laozi, Zhuangzi, Confucius and Mencius, and manifest themselves in the ideal of the Great Unity (大同). While the ways in which we understand freedom may differ, at its core are universal questions about how we understand ourselves, and how we relate to each other.

For some, it comes down to the relationship between authority and obedience. For others, freedom begins with an individual's ability to live with dignity. But, as with all of our most profound questions, there is no simple answer.

What it means to be free and to live in freedom changes with time and circumstance. In times of distress, when we feel threatened, we may forfeit more of our freedom in the hope of finding stability and strength within a collective. But remove that threat and our demand to live in freedom always reasserts itself. What matters is that we keep asking these questions. It is only with discussion and deliberation that we move closer to the truth as it is for our times.

Hong Kong, my home and the city that defined the person that I am today, is on the verge of becoming an authoritarian state. How did Asia's most liberal, open and cosmopolitan city, with a thriving civic society and institutions that were once seemingly so robust, change so fundamentally? How was a flourishing and free society undermined from within? What does it mean to be free in a world increasingly shaped by the rising authoritarian power of the People's Republic of China (PRC)?

This is not an academic book – it's not about abstract concepts, but about how freedom is felt and lived. For that reason, it is deeply personal. It is a reflection on the 'freedom' that is chanted on the streets and which inspires both hope and sacrifice. The word may mean different things to each of us, and it may pull on our hearts to different degrees, but we all wish to be free. We all need to be free.

In 2017, when I was twenty-four years old, I was convicted by a Hong Kong court for having incited and participated in an unlawful assembly. Three years earlier, I had called for a protest against the Hong Kong authorities that did not have their prior approval. Though the protest was peaceful, tensions were high. The court submission states that security guards were injured during scuffles, though no one was seriously hurt. No one was hospitalized, for which I am thankful. Certainly, it was never anyone's intention for anyone to be hurt.

It was 26 September 2014. I was on a hastily erected stage

at Civic Square, which was filling up with protestors. We had not applied for a permit for assembly because the protest had unfolded spontaneously. We also believed in our inherent right to protest. After all, we were only calling for the democratic reform we were promised under our own constitution. I called out, encouraging more people to enter the square and join us. Students, white-collar workers, activists and many others heeded the call, and as they climbed over the barriers that ringed the square, there was soon a large crowd. Spirits were high, and the scene, though chaotic, was also peaceful – we were energized, not angry.

Suddenly the lights were turned off and we were pitched into darkness. From among the assembled protestors a group of undercover police officers rushed up on to the stage. They surrounded me, grabbed my hands and declared that I was being arrested. I was pressed against the stage backdrop and could hardly move. As the police led me away through the crowds, shock soon turned to anger. Protestors sought to record what was happening with their phones. In response the police attempted to confiscate them. While police and protestors struggled, no one was intentionally assaulted by either side. Hong Kong had yet to lose its innocence.

I had broken the law. But I was also exercising freedoms of assembly and protest which are guaranteed under Hong Kong's constitution, known as the Basic Law. The protest itself was called because we wanted a fully elected legislature returned by universal suffrage, and to be able to vote for our Chief Executive, as the head of Hong Kong's government is called. This was the promise Beijing had made when Hong Kong was returned to Chinese sovereignty in 1997, and it is a promise that matters to Hong Kong people. So, to put it simply, I was jailed for asking Beijing to honour its word, to respect the constitution it had agreed for Hong Kong, and to treat Hong Kong people not as subjects but as citizens.

In July 2017, one month before my imprisonment, I was disqualified from my seat in Hong Kong's Legislative Council on orders from Beijing. That I had been elected to one of the Council's popularly contested seats and could therefore claim, unlike the majority of pro-Beijing legislators, to have a democratic mandate, only made me more of a target. Unable to persuade people not to give me their vote, the Chinese government chose instead to change the rules.

Within a year, and despite having sworn my oath of office to the word, my oath had been declared void and I was one of six pro-democracy legislators to be removed from the Council. A strong showing in the ballot had given us the numbers to block legislation requiring a two-thirds majority – the most power possible in a system rigged to favour Beijing's candidates. The six disqualifications happened to be exactly the number needed to swing the numbers back in Beijing's favour.

In the context of this political turmoil, and knowing that I was being targeted, I was anxious about my sentencing. Unlike in Mainland China, where the one-party dictatorship has a long and continuing history of political persecution, Hong Kong was meant to be different. In former Chinese leader Deng Xiaoping's famous phrase, we were supposed to be 'One Country, Two Systems' – two systems not only in our economy and in our structures of government, but in the way power is exercised. This model of governance was meant to preserve not only business confidence in the city, but also the values and way of life of a distinct and free Hong Kong community. Being sent to prison for a peaceful protest was new. It represented a worrying sign of how Hong Kong was changing.

My case, which was one of several that year, was the by-product of a deteriorating political climate marked by Beijing's increasing intervention in Hong Kong affairs, which had been steadily building over the past decade. Investment in Hong Kong had become leverage for economic control; and economic interest, coupled with political oversight, had increasingly corrupted Hong Kong's political and business elite. Most insidious was an attempt to reshape Hong Kong society to the values and narratives promoted by the Chinese Communist Party (CCP). That there was pushback from the people was not a surprise. That the Hong Kong authorities had now resorted to repressing their critics was shocking. A new chapter for Hong Kong had begun, and for activists like me jail became inevitable.

Sitting in the dock and listening to my verdict being read, I remember taking a deep breath to steady myself. It was surreal to be in this position – no matter how much you try to mentally prepare yourself, it's always hard to accept that you are going to be separated from your loved ones. I looked at my mother, who was in attendance at court alongside my friends. I saw her weeping.

My parents had divorced several years ago. While I regret that it had to be this way, I carry no resentment. I am particularly close to my mother. It was she who sheltered me, cared for me and raised me. To see that I, her youngest son, had become a cause of worry for her deeply affected me. I had only ever wanted her to be happy. Now I was the troublemaker sitting in the dock. As I faced jail that day, my mother, who in her heart knew that what I was doing was right, nevertheless faced her own form of penance. She continued to weep as the judge announced my eight-month sentence.

I told myself that such trials and tribulations were to be expected and vowed not to let it faze me. If I could get through these tests with a calm and open mind, and hold by my conscience, then I might have the right to call myself a true political activist. I did my best to remain positive about having to go to jail. However, prepared as I was for the verdict, I was nevertheless deeply affected when I heard the judgment read out in court.

Looking back, what shocked me most was the realization that laws which were supposed to enshrine our rights could, in the wrong hands, so easily turn into a tool of oppression. It made me question my faith that the legal system was there to protect the powerless. I had expected our right of assembly, my good character and the fact that I had no previous record to be weighed against what seemed to me a minor crime – one which essentially amounted to shouting encouragement to strangers. To jail me seemed disproportionate. But the government, it was now clear, was sending a signal.

The use of the law to serve the political agenda of autocracy, to suppress a peaceful protest that simply asked for government to be accountable to the people, left me horrified. This was not how it was supposed to be in Hong Kong, and the public took to the streets to make their feelings known. On 16 September 2019, 2 million people marched in protest in Hong Kong in support of freedom and the democratic movement. That's a quarter of the population. Many waited hours for trains and buses, then hours again lining the streets to reach the assembly point. More would no doubt have joined if they could.

Could any other cause inspire and mobilize so many people? Or have led so many people across the world to sacrifice their material betterment, personal liberty and even their lives in service of an ideal? Even when the aspiration is knocked back, as in Hong Kong, the desire to be free continues to burn strongly within us – it burns because freedom is central to our humanity.

My arrest and imprisonment were not onerous. Many have suffered far worse. But my case did set a precedent: in this new Hong Kong, unauthorized peaceful protest would be punished to the full measure of the law. I may now be at liberty, but only because I am in exile. In my absence the prison walls have grown to encompass the city that was my home. Life may continue on the surface, but a threat now hangs over anyone who dares simply to live by their conscience. Yet as long as I can stand with my people, wherever they may now be, and chant the same slogan calling for the freedoms and rights we were promised, I will. To call for the freedom of my people is not only just, it is right.

Hong Kong is the city I call home. It is the city to which I feel attached, the city I love. It has been my home and my community, and shaped the person I am today. In Hong Kong I have experienced happiness and love, disappointment and suffering. As I boarded a plane at Hong Kong International Airport for a life of exile in London, I knew I would never forget it.

Václav Havel, a former playwright and dissident, and the first president of the Czech Republic, wrote:

We never decided to become dissidents. We have been
transformed into them, without quite knowing how;
sometimes we have ended up in prison without precisely
knowing how. We simply went ahead and did certain things
that we felt we ought to do, and that seemed to us decent to
do, nothing more nor less.

It was never my intention to be an activist, to dedicate my life to fighting for freedom, democracy and justice. I never thought of myself as the troublemaker Beijing portrays me to be. It was its autocratic regime that forced me, and many others, to first stand up and speak out in defence of our liberties and our way of life. It is because they choose to rewrite our history and redefine our identity that we embrace our separate history and identity as Hongkongers. No one chooses to become a dissident. To dissent is a reaction.

As Milan Kundera aptly put it, 'The struggle of man against power is the struggle of memory against forgetting.' It is a struggle deeply embedded in China today. Power always wants the oppressed to look to the future, as the future is yet to be made. But we must remember, so that we can understand where we came from and imagine what might have been. In this book, I will tell you what happened to my Hong Kong over the past few years. *Freedom* is my struggle to remember what the CCP would have me forget. In telling it, I hope to show you how freedom is under threat everywhere, and teach you how to preserve your own freedoms before it's too late.

London, 2021

CHAPTER 1

FREEDOM, REFUGE AND HOPE

The warm glow of the sun on my mother's back. The image is seared deep into my memory. It is one of the few memories I have of my early life in Shenzhen, the booming Chinese city which borders Hong Kong.

Every day my mother would cycle me and my older brother to kindergarten. She rode a rusty bicycle with my brother sat up front and me at the back. A bicycle is not designed for three people, and it would have been easy to lose balance with children constantly running into the road, but that was all we had.

I clung tightly to my mother's waist as she rode. Sometimes I would turn my head to watch life go by as we cycled through bustling and chaotic neighbourhoods. Overhead a mass of wires and cables competed for space among washing lines, and children peered out from behind grilled windows at the streets below. Mostly, though, I just pressed my head firmly forward against my mother's back. Her body was both my anchor and a shelter from the world beyond. As the wind brushed past my cheeks, I would push myself ever more firmly up against her, holding her ever more tightly.

Though I was born in Shenzhen, I do not remember much of my life there. It is not a time we speak of much in the family. It is not a place I call home. All I can remember clearly are those bicycle rides through the city clinging to my mother's back. It was not the city but the bond I shared with my mother that mattered most.

The other childhood memory that left an indelible impression was of my coming to Hong Kong. It was 1999 and I was six years old. My father was already a resident, so we qualified under the Hong Kong government's reunion programme. When we arrived at Lo Wu Immigration Control Point, my mother ushered me forward. I would have to go through customs on my own as she prepared the necessary forms. In my hand she placed two bills, the first for fifty renminbi and the second for fifty Hong Kong dollars. It was the first time I realized Hong Kong and Mainland China had their own separate currencies.

It was the first sign of what I came to appreciate were the fundamental differences between the two. The border represented a change in education, language, culture and political system, but most importantly in values and in the way people think and behave. We were one country in name, but in reality we were more than just two systems – we were two distinct places, two peoples and two ways of life.

The two notes I was holding represented a small fortune to me. I put the money into my pocket and kept my hand pressed hard against my leg. It felt like a big responsibility, safeguarding the money my mother had given me as I embarked on this adventure, stepping into the unknown. I soon disappeared into the crowds, all heading to this city of which I heard so much on the news and from television – a city I would now be joining.

To understand how Hong Kong has changed, we have to begin by understanding the Hong Kong that was. This is not the Hong Kong of history books, or of national, colonial or corporate interests, but the Hong Kong that was lived by many of its people. The story of my parents is a good place to start.

City of Migrants

My parents are both from rural clan villages in Guangdong Province. Bordering Hong Kong to the south, Guangdong shares much in common with its neighbour. The provincial capital, Guangzhou, was historically known as Canton. The people of Guangdong are the Cantonese, and, as in Hong Kong, Cantonese is the native language. It is a relatively wealthy, rebellious and independently minded southern province of China.

As with all Chinese languages other than Mandarin Chinese, which is the basis of Putonghua or Guóyǔ (國語/国语), meaning 'national language', Cantonese is officially categorized by Beijing as a dialect. This is a political decision – among linguists the consensus is that Cantonese is a separate language. The two languages are not mutually understandable. As in Hong Kong, the Cantonese people have a distinct identity, and a long history of being on the fringe of imperial control.

To earn enough to provide for a family of five, my father decided to go and find work in Hong Kong. Like the millions who crossed the border, it was not a difficult choice.

A sampan, a small, flat-bottomed Chinese boat, carried my father across the border. It was a difficult journey and the people smugglers moved at night to avoid detection, which made the trip more perilous. Storms tossed many boats on to the oyster beds of Mirs Bay, their occupants thrown into shark-infested seas. It was not uncommon at the time for bodies to wash up on the shores of Hong Kong.

Why were people prepared to take such risks to get to Hong Kong? Partly it was economic. But it was also because, for many, Hong Kong represented freedom from the silent repression of Communist China. People feared hunger, but they also feared the vagaries and insecurity of the totalitarian system. Any day of your life, you might be denounced, even by your own family; everyone lived in fear of receiving that knock on the door, after which there was no recourse, let alone hope of justice.

After three nights on the boat with only moonlight to guide its path, my father arrived in Hong Kong. He was met on the shore, as arranged, by other members of our clan village who had made the journey before. He was exhausted. The passengers had shared the burden of rowing, and there had been precious little to eat or drink.

After a brief rest, my father had to make his way to the city centre, avoiding police patrols, to 'touch base'. For most of Hong Kong's history, people travelled freely between the colony and Mainland China, but with the establishment of the PRC in 1949 a hard border was erected. The British policy of allowing newcomers to touch base provided the flexibility for Hong Kong to legally integrate undocumented residents, while maintaining its side of the border. It allowed the city to continue to act as a safe haven for refugees fleeing political and social upheavals in China.

Keeping his head down and avoiding eye contact, my father made his way to his destination. Hong Kong was like a foreign land, with its seeming abundance, its freedoms and its Western fashions. And yet it was also a reassuringly Chinese city, making it the best of both worlds: free, open and distinctly Chinese. So my father and then his family, like so many of his generation, were granted right of residency.

My father worked as a construction worker while my mother remained in Mainland China with my two older brothers and me. Although I saw little of my father, it was through his hard work that we were able to put food on the table. This was a common set-up, the classic China–Hong Kong marriage, in which members of the family were physically separated but financially interconnected, the breadwinner bound to his higher wages in Hong Kong. Meanwhile, as often happened, my father applied for a one-way permit to allow us to emigrate to Hong Kong. His was a hard life, but, having lived through the madness of Mao's China, he was prepared to make the sacrifice if it meant his family might have the future he had been denied. Hong Kong was not only 'the land of gold', it was a place of freedom and security.

For my parents' generation, Hong Kong is not home in the way it is for my generation, who were raised and shaped in the city. For my parents, home continues to be our clan village. This connection to one's roots, reinforced by ancient clan customs, is important to them. However, I, and many of my generation, have only really known one home. We always took it for granted that we lived in an open society. The freedoms of Hong Kong shaped our values and our relationships. We placed a trust in society that my parents could never have imagined, and this trust was what allowed us to understand our rights and freedoms differently. We believe in our own agency, and that people should not only dare to imagine a better future, but work towards defining it and making it a reality. True, Hong Kong was not a democracy, but it had the rule of law. Information was not censored or controlled by the state. We were part of a thriving civil society. And our generation thought, perhaps naively, that the words of the authorities meant something, that promises for a more representative and democratic Hong Kong were made to be kept.

It is a great tragedy that so many of my generation, who were once able to look upon the PRC without the pain and cynicism of our parents' generation, are the ones who are now leaving. I never thought I would leave Hong Kong. I always thought I'd be buried there. But as my parents' generation know all too well, sometimes if we are to hold on to our values, we must let go of our other ties, even if that means leaving behind the only home we know.

It was a combination of idealism and viciousness that created the double nightmare of Mao's China – the Cultural Revolution and the Great Famine – compelling many ordinary men and women to seek refuge in Hong Kong. Due to Communist mismanagement, 30 million people are thought to have died of starvation, with a further 30 million unborn children aborted by their starving mothers. The violence of the Cultural Revolution killed 20 million more people. But most traumatizing for the Chinese people was the atmosphere of distrust and fear created by the regime. Neighbours turned on each other and children were encouraged to denounce their own parents for infractions of Party doctrine. Ideological fervour drove people to torture and kill. These events were without precedent, and served as a model for what would happen in Cambodia under the CCP-backed Khmer Rouge. They happened fifty years ago, but the collective trauma continues to shape the underlying psychology of many Chinese people today. To this day the CCP is unable to confront its own sins.

For many rural peasant families, the only hope was to be found in leaving their homeland. My father was one of the lucky ones to have reached safety in Hong Kong. Many never made it out of their village, their stories lost among the scores who simply disappeared. Though we never found wealth in Hong Kong, we were able to live our lives knowing we were part of a relatively just and stable society, and to sleep without fearing a knock on the door in the middle of the night. Hong Kong meant hope and survival. This is no longer the case. For those who escaped the terror of Mainland China, what is happening in Hong Kong now is all too familiar.

Why China's Aggression Matters

Freedom is our most fundamental human right. It is universal to us all. If the right to life is our right to exist, our right to be free allows us to live the only life worth living. We all need our own agency, freedom of thought and conscience. Without these we have no dignity.

Freedom should be the starting point for our relationships with others. To form and maintain those relationships we often choose to curtail our freedoms. We may relinquish a certain amount of freedom in return for collective benefits – for instance, I'm happy to give up some of my income in taxes so that I don't have to build my own roads or hospitals. We cede certain rights to government on the condition that it provides us with an environment in which we can live and, hopefully, prosper. This relationship between freedom and obedience is the basis of the social contract.

Freedom, and how we experience it, takes many shapes. For the North Korean defector, freedom may mean fleeing home. For people in extreme poverty, freedom may mean freedom from hunger. It all depends on the position we find ourselves in. Freedom, in practice, is never absolute. But we shouldn't confuse freedom with having a seeming abundance of choice.

In China, there are more than 2,000 television channels, and the programming seems diverse in style and content. But all programmes are made to conform to a single official narrative. We are not free to challenge this. This is fundamentally different to how life is in a free society, with freedom of information and a free press. In a free society, any restrictions to what we know and are allowed to know are dictated not by one political party's message but by basic social norms of decency to protect the vulnerable. For instance, young children aren't allowed to view violent or sexual content that might be traumatic for them. Freedom is restricted only to protect, and not to empower authority.

In China the press and media do not seek to report the truth or, really, to understand reality. They are there to promote a narrative. Often, in so doing, their role is to suppress the truth. The true meaning of freedom is not simply having a range of choices, but the ability to hold values and make choices that the ruling party does not like. As George Orwell put it, in a quote inscribed on the walls of Broadcasting House in London, the home of the BBC: 'If liberty means anything at all it means the right to tell people what they do not want to hear.'

Trade and globalization have brought more choice to liberal and illiberal countries alike, and on a superficial level the latter may feel more free. And yet for the first time, many, if not a majority of, people around the world are beholden to the whims of an authoritarian regime that tolerates no dissent. Where economic leverage had once been the means by which Hong Kong's limited freedoms were meant to be protected, today trade is used by China to apply pressure to reshape freedom around the world.

China is fighting a war of ideals with the free world. Xi Jinping has made it clear that everything in China must serve the Party, and he is willing to weaponize every relationship, whether cultural, academic, media or business, to execute the Party's agenda. As China has become more assertive, it has begun to compel companies and individuals not only to accept its political interests but to lobby on behalf of them, even when that means betraying our conscience and under-mining our own freedoms.[*]

In October 2019, during the height of the anti-extradition protest in Hong Kong, Daryl Morey, at that time the general manager of the Houston Rockets, an American National Basketball Association (NBA) team, voiced his personal support for the Hong Kong protests.[†] He had been following developments in Hong Kong closely and was perfectly within his rights as an American citizen, in America, to express his opinion. However, after the Chinese state boycotted broadcasts of the NBA, he was forced to retract his statement. A spokesperson for the Chinese Consulate-General in Houston had urged the Rockets to 'correct the error'.[‡] As the NBA's commissioner Adam Silver summed it up two weeks after the incident, 'The financial consequences have been and may continue to be fairly dramatic.'[§]

The same month Daryl Morey made his comments, Ng Wai Chung (吳偉聰), a leading Hong Kong e-sports player, who goes by the name Blitzchung, was expelled from a gaming tournament hosted by Blizzard Entertainment, an

---

[*]   'China Bullies Foreign Companies into Espousing Its Worldview', https://www.nationalreview.com/2018/06/china-bullies-foreign-companies-into-espousing-its-worldview

[†]   'Daryl Morey backtracks after Hong Kong tweet causes Chinese backlash', https://www.bbc.com/news/business-49956385

[‡]   'Houston Rockets GM apologizes for Hong Kong tweet after China consulate tells team to "correct the error"', https://www.cnbc.com/2019/10/07/houston-rockets-gm-morey-deletes-tweet-about-hong-kong.html

[§]   '"The Losses Have Already Been Substantial." Adam Silver Addresses Fallout From the NBA-China Controversy', https://time.com/5703259/adam-silver-nba-china-time-100-health-summit

American games developer. He was forced to forfeit all the prize money he had won so far (approximately $4,000) and was banned from other professional events for a year. His offence was to have expressed in an interview his personal support for the Hong Kong protest movement.[*]

The outcome this time was very different. In response to the ban, many gamers and fans around the world created #BoycottBlizzard, which gained significant support, including from employees at Blizzard Entertainment. US Senators Ron Wyden and Marco Rubio initiated a campaign of their own that received cross-party support, with Representatives Alexandria Ocasio-Cortez, Mike Gallagher and Tom Malinowski among others signing a letter calling on Blizzard to reverse their decision. Under pressure, Blizzard did so several days later.

These are only two in a whole catalogue of examples of how China is willing to use economic blackmail to silence fundamental freedoms, not only within China but around the world. This is not about protecting the Chinese people from foreign 'bad influence' – people in China are prevented from obtaining objective perspectives about the outside world anyway. It is about China's intolerance of dissent anywhere, seeking not only to promote 'understanding' of China but to control what we know and are allowed to think.

Companies will often justify censorship by claiming they are against the expression of any political opinion. But when

---

[*] 'Blizzard Entertainment Bans Esports Player After Pro-Hong Kong Comments', https://www.npr.org/2019/10/08/768245386/blizzard-entertainment-bans-esports-player-after-pro-hong-kong-comments?t=1621279560445

a whole civilization becomes the domain of one political party – when, as Beijing says, only the CCP can represent the Chinese people, and to love China is to love the Party – everything about China becomes political. Unlike in democratic countries, there is no distinction between what is political and what is not political, nor between Party and state. In such a situation, companies don't have the luxury of simply sitting back and claiming to be apolitical.

Cathay Pacific, Hong Kong's flagship airline, discovered how far the rules had changed when in 2019 Beijing threatened to close Chinese airspace, effectively grounding the airline, unless the company provided the authorities with a list of all staff who had, in their personal capacity, shown support for the protests. The company was also asked to take disciplinary action against such staff. Simply leaving a personal message of support on social media was deemed unacceptable. When Cathay's Chief Executive Officer, Rupert Hogg, refused and 'reportedly sent the authorities a list with only one name on it, his own', he was forced out and the company management was changed.* Cathay's parent company, Swire Pacific, is a British conglomerate. This does not matter: neutrality is no longer an option.

China is increasingly undermining our freedoms in other areas too. Universities across the free world are facing up to the challenge of Chinese-state-backed harassment of anyone who speaks up against the regime. Chinese Students and

---

*   'Cathay CEO resigns amid Hong Kong protest blowback as more rallies planned', https://www.reuters.com/article/us-hongkong-protests-idUSKCN1V6o6U

Scholars Associations, reporting directly to Chinese embassies, actively monitor campuses.* Controversial 'Confucius Institutes', affiliated to the Party, are in some cases replacing independent Chinese language and culture departments. They may not be designed to openly indoctrinate students, but they do seek to shape the discourse on China within universities. Departments that once sought to understand China for what it is are being replaced by ones that promote the Party narrative.†

Academics and students alike are routinely threatened online, as are their families. For budding academics and researchers, career progress has in many areas become dependent on having the right 'mindset' to work with the CCP, which has been allowed through its proxies to fund research and endow professorships. Oxford University has started teaching its students of China according to Chatham House Rules – information from meetings can be shared, but not the identities of participants – to avoid students being targeted by the Chinese state.‡ Others have followed suit, or implemented their own guidelines and policies to protect Hong Kong and Chinese students, and their families in

---

* 'China's long arm reaches into American campuses', https://foreignpolicy .com/2018/03/07/chinas-long-arm-reaches-into-american-campuses-chinese-students-scholars-association-university-communist-party

† 'It's time for Western universities to cut their ties to China', https:// foreignpolicy.com/2020/08/19/universities-confucius-institutes-china; see also https://www.bbc.co.uk/news/world-asia-china-49511231

‡ 'Oxford moves to protect students from China's Hong Kong security law', https://www.theguardian.com/education/2020/sep/28/oxford-moves-to-protect-students-from-chinas-hong-kong-security-law

China, from possible retribution for exploring ideas (which is, after all, the whole point of academia).[*]

It's no exaggeration to say that democracy itself has come under threat. The case of former Senator Sam Dastyari, who was accused by then Australian prime minister Malcolm Turnbull of accepting money in exchange for supporting China in its South China Sea territorial disputes, led Australia to become the first country to look seriously at Chinese infiltration and attempted manipulation of its democracy. All across the democratic world, from New Zealand to Switzerland, from the US to the UK, the work of China's United Front Department in undermining our societies and democratic systems from within has been exposed. Chinese embassies have also seen no problem with instructing local politicians and political parties to silence people within their own parties, including allegedly asking for troublesome individuals to be removed from the lists of electoral candidates.[†]

We cannot brush this off as part of the usual game of international politics. China is attracting special attention, alongside Russia, because it oversteps established lines, and because it is pioneering new ways of operating in a 'grey zone'. A decade ago, some people might naively have presumed that China was converging on accepted standards. The argument was

---

[*] 'UK university tells lecturers not to record classes about Hong Kong and China, citing security law risks', https://hongkongfp.com/2021/05/10/uk-university-tells-lecturers-not-to-record-classes-about-hong-kong-and-china-citing-security-law-risks

[†] 'Boris Johnson's Conservatives Are Burning Bridges With China', https://www.bloomberg.com/news/articles/2020-11-25/boris-johnson-s-conservative-party-is-burning-bridges-with-china

that, if we gave in to the demands of the CCP in the short term, China's engagement with international institutions would shape the country for the better. This did not mean that China had to be more like the West, but rather that as a mature state it would respect and adhere to the common set of norms the rest of us do. That view, we can now see, was rose-tinted at best. The reality is that China is growing more authoritarian and more demanding. Faced with only mild resistance, it is becoming ever more sensitive to slights, more emboldened to act and more aggressive in pursuing anyone who does not agree with its world view.

Already the world's second-largest economy, China is forecast by some to overtake the US as the largest by 2028.[*] For the first time in modern history, the world's biggest economy will be an authoritarian one-party state. It asserts itself not only from a position of strength, but with the aggression of a state that has spent generations instilling in its people a sense of national humiliation and victimization.[†] China's regime not only doesn't respect democratic freedoms, but openly declares them a threat. And it no longer pretends to abide by international rules, aiming to shape the international order itself.

It is easy to forget how hard-fought and how fragile our freedoms really are. Our freedom of conscience is threatened when, like Morey, we are prevented from expressing our

[*] 'Chinese economy to overtake US "by 2028" due to COVID-19', https://www.bbc.co.uk/news/world-asia-china-55454146
[†] 'Never forget national humiliation: Historical memory in Chinese politics and foreign relations', https://academic.oup.com/ahr/article-abstract/120/3/994/19901

support for a cause we believe to be just. Our freedom of thought is impaired when we are punished for engaging with human rights, or discussing the future of Taiwan and Hong Kong. Most insidious is when we stop noticing the way these restrictions are being imposed on us, and begin to parrot the talking points of a political party. We owe it to ourselves to safeguard our freedoms, and to stand firmly by them when they are threatened.

But when our freedoms are restricted unjustly and without our consent, we feel the loss. We feel it as oppression and injustice.

When our constitutional right to peaceful assembly in Hong Kong was banned, simply to protect the veneer of legitimacy of an unelected and unaccountable government, I felt as if the air had been sucked out of my lungs. I felt heavy and disorientated. Most of all, I felt powerless.

In 2019, during the early stages of the protests, I would sometimes find myself standing on the front line between protestors and the police. Witnessing the clashes, what struck me most was the imbalance in physical power between the two sides. The police were in full riot gear, armed and armoured, with firearms, batons and shields; and the protestors, mostly young, sometimes school-aged children, had only goggles and yellow plastic helmets for protection. Many carried small backpacks for water, wet towels, sometimes a little food or some basic first aid gear. Movingly, some had taken to carrying a note to their families or lawyers, should they fall victim to a beating or arrest. A few even carried a goodbye note. It was shocking to know that there were Hong Kong people who felt they might be killed by their own police force, once a source of pride as 'Asia's finest' – the very police who were supposed to be protecting them.

In their notes, protestors often apologized to their families and loved ones for the worry they had caused.

'I am so worried about dying, and I may not be able to see you again. I [am] worried that you will cry for me, [and] collapse, but it's impossible for me to hide from the street protests.'

'I actually worry that I will die and won't see you any more.'

'I worry that you will cry and feel devastated. But there is no way that I won't take to the streets.'

A *New York Times* report documented the content of the last letter from an anonymous twenty-two-year-old front-line protester who called himself 'nobody':*

'Dad, I'm unfilial for leaving you so early, before I could fulfil my obligations as a son, to be there for you.'

Others read:

'When I'm gone, please take good care of yourself.'

---

* 'In Hong Kong, Gasoline Bombs, Masks and . . . Goodbye Letters', https://www.nytimes.com/2019/10/20/world/asia/hong-kong-protesters-letters.html

'I would be lying if I told you that I'm not afraid. But of course, we cannot give up.'

It is both moving and inspiring to discover how deeply so many people felt the need to protest. It had begun to seem as if protest was the only way we could fight to preserve the freedoms and the values of our home. The responsibility weighed on us: many expressed feelings of guilt and disappointment, that they felt compelled to take to the streets as all other avenues had been exhausted. No one forced them to protest or to put their lives at risk, and yet they did, in their hundreds of thousands. It was their conscience that drove them.

These are the people that Beijing and its Hong Kong government apologists sought to portray as hooligans – delinquent youths and troublemakers acting without a thought for their families. On the contrary: many protestors I have met know they are making a sacrifice. Many live stable and comfortable lives and are successful in what they do. Materially they have nothing to gain from rocking the boat – in fact, they have much to lose. Yet they are prepared to lend their voice to the chorus.

All over the world where people feel oppressed, whether in Belarus, Thailand or Myanmar, they are willing to risk everything to fight for their rights. It is not because they put themselves first, but rather because they believe in doing their part to create a just and free society. Perhaps this makes freedom sound like a lofty ideal, but I think freedom is as much a gut feeling as a thought – as much a cause of the heart as of the head. What drives their pursuit of freedom is not only the ideal, but also their revulsion against the opposite – to be unfree. It is their sense of being oppressed, of witnessing or experiencing injustice and unfairness, that is the driver.

In injustice we find a cause for action, and for exceptional strength and courage. We find the best in our nature – empathy, selflessness and a sense of community, as I saw in 2014 during the Umbrella Movement, when hundreds of thousands of young people occupied major highways to demand democracy. Strangers cared for each other, looked out for each other, shared all that they had for the betterment of the community. Standing up together for what we believe, and even suffering together, unites us in ways nothing else can.

That's why the identity of 'Hongkonger' is so important, and has only become stronger the more China has sought to suppress it. It no longer simply denotes people with a shared experience of life in a city we call home: among the majority who support the protests it has come to represent a shared experience of suffering and pain that is unique to our circumstances. When you begin to see others in your community as brothers and sisters, you care for them as family and you find the will to make any sacrifice.

From Refuge to Persecutor

On the morning of 17 August 2017, when I was due to appear at court, I woke up later than usual. I lay on my bed with my two pet cats. They were rescues – which only made me feel I had to love them more. As I stroked them, I could feel them react to me, their bodies relax. They purred in that loving way only cats do, making a sound that seemed to vibrate with emotion. They did not know I was saying goodbye.

I wanted to remember the exact feeling of being on my bed – the texture of the mattress, and the way it shaped itself to my body as I lay there. Like most flats in Hong Kong, mine was little more than a bedroom. But it was my first home away from my family. And I would not see it again.

The landlord had kindly allowed me to terminate my rental agreement early. This is unusual in Hong Kong. I suspected he may have privately been sympathetic to my situation and to the cause I was fighting for. Most people are, though many dare not say so. My family would come when I had gone to pack up my things and ensure the flat was ready to be returned. I couldn't help but wonder who might live there after me, and whether the new tenants would know my story, why I had left so suddenly. I suspected they would. But life goes on in Hong Kong, no matter the hardship.

Detainees are not allowed shoelaces at the detention centre, so I chose to wear a pair of sneakers. I was immediately escorted to the detention room at the court once the verdict was given. Time passed slowly. The room was cold and sterile. The harshness of the environment and its lack of humanity affected me. I spotted a glimmer of sunlight through the window and imagined the warmth of its rays on my skin, if only it could reach me. I thought of my family, searching my memories to build up a presence I felt I needed but was missing – how it felt to hold them, and the way my mother's eyes could express to me everything she could not say.

When I was released from prison in October 2017, I was a changed man. An innocence had gone. Hong Kong was no longer what it was to me when I arrived as a child. It is not that it was any less my home – in fact, it meant more to me then than it ever had. But I knew, though I was now supposedly a free man, that the shackles remained, invisible now but all the worse for it. The fear of living in an unfree city may not be physically constraining in the way a prison is, but it is no less restricting to the mind. I worried about the terrible things that might happen to my friends simply for holding an opinion. I imagined them facing trumped-up charges of election rigging or of failing the election vetting process. So many activists had endured such persecution and ended up in jail or in exile. When the lines around what constitutes a crime begin to blur, your imagination becomes your own worst enemy.

The Hong Kong I knew may have felt free from day to day, but without democratic representation its institutions were built on sand. Our way of life depended on politicians understanding and respecting our values and freedoms, and acknowledging the unique nature of our history. But nothing obliged them to respect us, and when Beijing asserted its grip Hong Kong's freedoms sank quickly. As it is, Hong Kong's Chief Executive, the leader of the city's government, is indirectly appointed by the CCP. Selected by Beijing, elected by a body controlled by Beijing, and then confirmed by Beijing before taking office, the Hong Kong government is accountable to and serves only the CCP. In this system, the government need not concern itself with the view from the street. Without democracy, freedoms are not ours by right, but for authorities to bestow.

In the colonial era, even though the governors of Hong

Kong were not elected, they were at least appointed by a government with a democratic mandate. They shared our values and understood and respected what it meant to live in an open and free society. The British left us with the means to ensure justice through an unbiased court system and to seek some level of accountability through a free press. The Chinese government is a one-party dictatorship. It is unelected and unaccountable. It tolerates no criticism or opposition. Even limited freedoms are treated as a threat to the Party's uncontested authority.

Since 2014, the speed at which Hong Kong's freedoms have been eroded has been dramatic. Britain, which has declared four 'clear and serious' breaches of the 1984 Sino–British Joint Declaration, now considers China to be in a state of 'ongoing non-compliance'.* It is a position echoed by many in the international community, including the US, Canada, Australia and the EU,† all of whom now recognize that the city is no longer sufficiently autonomous to warrant the special treatment it once enjoyed. The US no longer extends special trading rights to Hong Kong,‡ and many nations have

---

* 'Foreign Secretary statement on radical changes to Hong Kong's electoral system', https://www.gov.uk/government/news/foreign-secretary-statement-on-radical-changes-to-hong-kongs-electoral-system

† 'Hong Kong: Declaration by the High Representative on behalf of the EU on the electoral system', https://www.consilium.europa.eu/en/press/press-releases/2021/03/11/hong-kong-declaration-by-the-high-representative-on-behalf-of-the-eu-the-electoral-system

‡ 'Trump Ends Hong Kong's Special Status With US to Punish China', https://www.bloomberg.com/news/articles/2020-07-14/trump-to-address-china-tensions-in-tuesday-rose-garden-event

ended extradition treaties with the city since human rights can no longer be guaranteed.*

Perhaps the worst single development was on 30 June 2020, when the Chinese government imposed on Hong Kong its new National Security Law (NSL). Beijing broke its treaty obligations in doing so. All Hong Kong authorities, including the government and the legislature, were circumvented. There was no consultation process. The law was enacted by decree, as if applying the mandate of heaven.

The NSL covers the crimes of secession (seeking to break away from China), subversion (undermining the power or authority of the central government), terrorism and collusion with foreign forces, but defines them so vaguely as to leave them open to political interpretation and give the authorities sweeping powers to arrest people. Inciting hatred of the Chinese or Hong Kong governments has been criminalized, and merely spray-painting government property may now be classed as terrorism. The law, according to Beijing, will help restore stability to Hong Kong – not by addressing the underlying reasons for our discontent, but by putting its hand over our mouths.

In the days following its implementation, the police arrested and sought to charge people under this new law for

---

* 'Hong Kong Watch welcomes Ireland and the Netherlands decision to suspend its extradition treaty with Hong Kong and calls for EU Members to now go further and suspend extradition with China', https://www .hongkongwatch.org/all-posts/2020/10/23/hong-kong-watch-welcomes-irelands-decision-to-suspend-its-extradition-treaty-with-hong-kong-and-calls-for-eu-members-to-now-go-further-and-suspend-extradition-with-china

chanting slogans. To say 'Free Hong Kong' is now a serious criminal offence. People are being arrested for the possession of stickers.

Mainland law enforcement officers now operate in Hong Kong, unaccountable to the Hong Kong authorities. Those arrested under the new laws may face trial by a politically appointed judge, with no jury, and could face jail on the Mainland. In all these ways, the National Security Law is a violation of rights supposedly protected under the Sino–British Joint Declaration and by Hong Kong's Basic Law, and is actually unconstitutional under Chinese law. Yet even during this most bitter of times, the spirit of ordinary Hong Kong people continues to shine, even if it must do so in the shadows.

We may not again witness the mass protests of the past, but individual acts of defiance continue. In the face of oppression and injustice, the flame of freedom and our desire for democracy only burns more deeply in our hearts. The greater the challenge, the greater the human spirit that rises to meet it. The experience of losing freedoms we once took for granted has been truly terrible, yet in the process many Hongkongers have rediscovered what is most important. By continuing to struggle we will continue to feel free. As long as we fight, there remains hope that justice will prevail.

I left Shenzhen as a young child for a better life and for the greater freedoms of Hong Kong. The hope among many at that time, in China and across the world, had been that in time China would become more like Hong Kong. Instead, today Hong Kong is becoming more like China. If I were to return to Shenzhen today, which I am unable to do, I would see many pictures of President Xi hung around the city;

slogans declaring China a champion of such ideas as 'democracy', the 'rule of law' and, yes, even 'freedom'. A parallel universe is being created where all meanings are twisted to have 'Chinese characteristics'. And while China may be remarkably more affluent than it was twenty years ago, it remains a very different place to Hong Kong.

It is different because the values that underpin its society are different. There was once a time in China's recent history when one saw the same hope and determination in people's eyes in both Hong Kong and on the Mainland; when Chinese people around the world were united in a common dream to be not only prosperous but also free. That time blossomed in May 1989, when across China millions of ordinary people came out in peaceful protest to demand that economic liberalization be accompanied by political liberalization. They did not wish to overthrow the Party, only that the Party and the system would evolve. In June 1989, as we will explore later, this flame of hope was extinguished on the Mainland with tanks and gunfire. However, despite crackdowns, the nationalist education system and campaigns of historic revisionism, it continues to burn in the hearts of Chinese people, buried, perhaps, but not extinguished. Life is about more than the economy and our material well-being, or narrow ideas of nationalism. A country that does not allow its people to be free can only ever be poor; the spark of humanity, of human potential, is missing.

To me, as long as Hong Kong people fight for what they were promised and what they deserve, the spirit that made that city my home will continue to live. The fire may not burn brightly on the horizon, but knowing that somewhere the flame is alive is what gives us hope.

CHAPTER 2

THE EROSION OF FREEDOM

The Hong Kong Story

As a British colony, Hong Kong was where many of Asia's nationalist and anti-colonial movements found refuge and the space to organize. Its relative freedoms meant that radical newspapers could be printed, people mobilized and funds collected. For Hong Kong's British administrators, the priority was trade, not ideology. As long as stability and good diplomatic relations were not endangered, laissez-faire colonial rule meant the people themselves were not imposed upon by the authorities. It was not a crime to hold or express a political opinion, nor to be openly critical of the authorities.

It is sometimes said by those who wish to deny Hongkongers their freedoms that Hong Kong has never been free, and that the British never granted them the political freedoms now being demanded of Beijing. On one level this is true: Hong Kong people have always been denied the

opportunity to choose their own government without outside interference. It is also true that, whether as part of China
or as a British colony, Hong Kong has only ever been part of
an empire. But the picture is not that simple.

For Britain, the Crown Colony of Hong Kong had become
an expense Britain could ill afford (it was not until the 1980s
that the colony paid for itself). In London it was also increasingly seen as an embarrassing relic; it had been expected that
Beijing would demand the return of Hong Kong when the
Communists took power in China in 1949. Should China
demand Hong Kong, Britain was powerless to prevent it.

When this did not happen, Britain suggested that Hong
Kong might be granted self-government and Dominion status, as had happened with Singapore. This would have been
consistent with evolving colonial thinking. However, Zhou
Enlai, in a conversation with a British official in 1958, made
Beijing's position clear: any attempt by Britain to grant self-
government to Hong Kong would be considered a 'very
unfriendly act'. When, in the 1960s and with US backing, the
British once more raised the issue of even limited self-
government in the colony, Chinese officials were again
unambiguous in their response: as they made clear to Hong
Kong union representatives, China's leaders would 'not hesi-
tate to take positive action to have Hong Kong, Kowloon and
the New Territories liberated'.*

The difference between outspoken Hong Kong society
and authoritarian China became increasingly apparent. Under

---

* 'The secret history of Hong Kong's stillborn democracy', https://
qz.com/279013/the-secret-history-of-hong-kongs-stillborn-democracy

Mao Zedong (毛澤東), the PRC had become a totalitarian state which intervened in every aspect of life and demanded not only obedience but submission to official orthodoxy. Britain, by contrast, was coming to terms with the end of its own empire. As Maoist orthodoxy stifled the Mainland, Hong Kong's values were orienting in a different direction entirely. In 1964, the year China conducted its first nuclear test in Xinjiang, the newspapers in Hong Kong reported: 'Hundreds of screaming teenagers in Hong Kong yesterday gave Britain's Beatles a wild welcome.'*

What frightened Beijing was the development of a political alternative in the colony that might challenge the Party's claim to represent all Chinese. Meanwhile, the continuing colonial status of Hong Kong also served the Party's economic interests by providing a way for China to access markets that were otherwise closed to them, at a time when the domestic economy was tightly controlled by the state. For Britain, while this was not ideal, it was not prepared to risk its own commercial interests in the city.

Hong Kong may not have had self-government, but at least it was administered and governed by those who understood and valued freedom, even if they were not in a position to grant the political freedoms Hong Kong lacked. While political rights were suppressed, Hong Kong nevertheless continued to benefit from the trappings of an increasingly free and open society, in line with developments elsewhere in

---

* 'When The Beatles came to Hong Kong in June 1964, and screaming teenagers welcomed the Fab Four at Kai Tak airport', https://www.scmp .com/magazines/post-magazine/short-reads/article/2096509/when- beatles-came-hong-kong-june-1964-and

the free world. It enjoyed freedom of expression, a flourishing and free press and the rule of law. A professional civil service served an executive that may not have been elected, but was nevertheless drawn from a democratic tradition and understood the need to be accountable. Hong Kong residents could write to Members of Parliament in London to express their concerns, and did so. In this way, issues such as corruption in the colonial administration and child labour were raised by the community and addressed.

Freedoms rely not only on systems, but on a mindset. The British administrators who governed Hong Kong were drawn from a society with a long tradition of freedom. They understood and valued human rights. They were also, as colonial administrators, acutely aware that their exercise of power lacked legitimacy. Therefore they were generally cautious, instinctively seeking to balance interests rather than take sides. This was most notable in the way the colonial administration handled the competing political loyalties of the CCP, the Nationalists (Kuomintang, in Taiwan) and the British Crown. Colonial officers, who often spoke the local dialect, prized the relationships they developed in the local community. Even today it is not uncommon to find people who remember these relationships. This meant that Hong Kong was governed not by what London or Beijing believed ought to happen, but in light of the actual situation on the ground.

In the late 1960s and 1970s, before beginning negotiations with Beijing on Hong Kong's future, the British colonial government sought to establish the city as a financial centre of regional importance. By making Hong Kong economically important to China, Britain hoped this would give them leverage in negotiating on Hong Kong's behalf. It would also be a way to better equip Hong Kong to ride out the potential turmoil of being handed back to a Communist country, as well as helping to entrench British economic interests in the city. Hong Kong would be not only the 'goose that laid the golden eggs' but also act as a bridge for China to access global markets and capital. In 1949 the decline of Shanghai, historically China's commercial and financial centre, had left Hong Kong ideally placed to take on this role.

To transform Hong Kong into an international financial centre, the city had to be attractive to foreign capital and investment. The rule of law and the free flow of information, movement and capital, as well as the protection of private properties and assets, provided firm foundations on which the city's economy would be built.

To attract foreign talent, investments were also made in developing the city socially and culturally. By the 1980s Hong Kong had its own distinct civil society, with an indigenous Hong Kong–Chinese community identity. In a city that had for much of its history been defined by migrants and refugees, a new generation arose that identified with Hong Kong as home. Hongkongers increasingly saw themselves as distinct from Mainland Chinese, with their own cultural, ideological and historical roots. This Hong Kong identity was perfectly compatible with being Chinese – in fact, for many it was Hong Kong that was preserving an 'authentic' and unpoliticized Chinese identity separate from the Communist Party.

It was not until the start of the 1980s, during the negotiations between Britain and China on Hong Kong's return to

Chinese administration, that political representation again became an issue. Hong Kong, no longer merely a refuge but a place where people had put down roots, had changed, and political rights were increasingly becoming a matter of concern for the city's expanding middle classes. Fears rather than ideals drove the politicization of the Hong Kong people, who worried that the freedoms they currently enjoyed would be eroded by authoritarian China. This led to the first of several waves of emigration in which hundreds of thousands left Hong Kong, mostly to Canada and Australia. Many residents had already fled repression in Communist China and were fully aware of what Beijing was capable of. Beijing, however, was insistent that Hong Kong people were to have no voice in deciding their own future.

China had never recognized British sovereignty in Hong Kong, which had come about through the 'unequal treaties' forced upon the Qing Empire by the British a century before. Britain was understood to be merely administering Hong Kong. In Beijing's eyes, neither Britain nor the people of Hong Kong had any legitimacy to make demands of Beijing in negotiating the territories' return to Chinese administration. Hong Kong's people were, so to speak, already Chinese and therefore already represented by the CCP. Thus, despite protestations from the British, Hongkongers were excluded from negotiations on the future of Hong Kong and denied a say in their own future.

The negotiations on Hong Kong's future led to the Sino–British Joint Declaration, a legally binding treaty registered with the United Nations. Britain agreed to renounce its sovereignty over Hong Kong and the Kowloon Peninsula, which encompasses the city of Hong Kong, upon the expiration of the New Territories lease in 1997. In return, China agreed to preserve Hong Kong's freedoms, its separate political, economic and legal institutions, and its way of life under the 'One Country, Two Systems' formula. This would last for at least fifty years, that is until 2047, and would be renewable.

The agreement was in the interests of both parties. Britain was offered a way to withdraw from a colonial commitment that was no longer strategically necessary nor politically defensible. In so doing it could close its own imperial chapter with dignity and the conclusion that it had been, at least in Hong Kong, a force for good. For China, the handover represented the correction of what it regarded as a historic wrong, thus closing the door on a humiliating period in Chinese history. The Chinese guarantees prevented the ignominy of a British withdrawal that surrendered its colonial subjects to an authoritarian power. By the same token, the deal allowed Beijing to present Hong Kong's 'return to the motherland' as a significant step towards its own national project of reuniting China, and to avoid the awkward question as to whether this was what the Hong Kong people actually wanted.

Following this agreement, in 1984 the Hong Kong colonial government published a Green Paper on the Further Development of Representative Government in Hong Kong. Political parties were permitted, and the first indirect Legislative Council election was held in 1985, with direct elections following in 1991. This was a reflection of changing times. At the Eleventh National Congress of the Communist Party of China, Deng Xiaoping had repudiated the Cultural Revolution and was now steering China towards opening up to the world. China was beginning to liberalize its economy. It had a new constitution (1982) that, at least on paper, recognized and protected human rights. Easing restrictions meant that China, while still a highly authoritarian state, began to see the emerging signs of civil society. Many hoped that Hong Kong would be the vanguard that paved the way towards a more free and democratic China.

Events in 1989 in Tiananmen Square in Beijing, and across the country, later shattered this dream. The suppression of the protests deeply affected people in Hong Kong. Many now chose to leave, with those who could afford it moving to the US, the UK, Canada and Australia. Trust in the CCP, which had at the best of times been fragile, was broken. It was a harsh reminder that the priority for Beijing was not the people of China but the preservation of the Party.

John Major, the UK prime minister, was the first world leader to visit Beijing when it was left out in the diplomatic cold after 1989. One of his chief concerns was the smooth transfer of sovereignty, and Britain sought to ease fears by introducing in 1990 the Basic Law that would soon become the constitution of the Hong Kong Special Administrative Region (HKSAR). While the Sino–British Joint Declaration guaranteed that Hong Kong's existing institutions and freedoms would not be curtailed, the Basic Law enshrined a commitment by Beijing towards further democratic reform. Articles 2 and 3 of the Basic Law state that the 'ultimate aim' is for the Chief Executive and legislature to be elected by universal suffrage in accordance with democratic procedures.

The significance of this was not lost on Chris Patten, the last Governor of Hong Kong (1992–7). Unusually, he was not a diplomat but a politician, and he was prepared to rock the diplomatic boat if it meant doing right by the Hong Kong people. Despite angering both Beijing and local business elites, he insisted on initiating discussions on constitutional reform before his term was over. He was told categorically that Hongkongers were not political and that democracy was a Western ideal that meant nothing to the ordinary people. This was not, however, what he heard on the street, and surveys consistently showed high levels of support for his proposals. In 1994 his reform package carried in the Hong Kong legislature, significantly increasing democratic representation. In the 1994 District Board elections and 1995 Legislative Council elections, pro-democracy candidates swept the board.

Beijing condemned Patten as a 'Sinner of a Thousand Years' (千古罪人).* To Sir Percy Cradock, Britain's former Ambassador to China and the architect of Britain's policy towards the PRC, he had 'made himself so obnoxious to the Chinese' that he endangered the deal already struck. Cradock, who was officer-in-charge at the British Embassy in Beijing when it was stormed by a Leftist mob in 1967, was instinctively aware of the weakness of Britain's position. The Chinese leaders were 'thuggish dictators', Cradock argued, but could be 'trusted to do what they promise'.

Despite dividing opinion between those driven by a desire for democracy and the more 'pragmatic' pro-China lobby, Patten left office significantly more popular than any of the

---

* 'Patten: liberal treatment of China's infamy', http://news.bbc.co.uk/chinese/trad/hi/newsid_1910000/newsid_1910800/1910806.stm

Chief Executives who would replace him. It's worth remembering that many of those patriotic pro-China voices would still wish to be free. The difference is that their public position, like Cradock's, is driven less by their dreams than by their fears.

Despite Patten's efforts, 1997 nevertheless marked the end of any hope that the territory would secure a democratic system before the handover of sovereignty. The Union Jack was lowered for the last time over Hong Kong, and the Five-starred Red Flag of the PRC rose to replace it. On the streets of Hong Kong crowds gathered to witness history. And yet the mood was far from joyous. The overwhelming majority of people did not feel liberated from the shackles of colonial oppression. So, despite the carefully stage-managed scene, the defining mood was one of fear – the territory might be semi-autonomous, but the other half of that equation was an authoritarian state. The questions on the minds of many were: would the 'high degree of autonomy' guaranteed by Beijing in the Sino–British Joint Declaration be enough to guarantee our way of life? Would 'Hong Kong people rule Hong Kong'? And, for the many families who had suffered under the CCP, could Beijing be trusted to honour its word?

Many Hongkongers whose families had already fled the CCP once felt that Beijing simply could not be trusted. History shows that they were right: Beijing refused to recognize those elected under Patten's reforms and immediately rolled back his changes. New questions were now raised, not least: how did Beijing understand universal suffrage and democratic procedure?

For most Hongkongers, life went on as it had done before.

As locals would say, the 'horse races and dancing' continued and lives remained seemingly unchanged. Within a few years, though, signs of change were beginning to show. The economy became increasingly dependent on China, and eroded Hong Kong's ability to withstand political pressure from Beijing. More sinister were changes to the way in which key Hong Kong institutions began to function. The press, once the most vibrant and free in Asia, was being co-opted through its ownership and through strategic appointments. Self-censorship became an increasing problem. This was particularly chilling for a city with such diverse (mostly Chinese) identities. Newspapers shifted subtly from being a means of community expression to one of imposing compliance. Increasingly, Hong Kong's identity, which the British had left to the people to define in their own way, was being overwritten by Beijing. In schools, mother-tongue learning seamlessly switched, without consultation, from Cantonese to Putonghua. A previously inclusive identity was replaced by appeals to 'love China, love Hong Kong'. Suddenly, 'China' meant not our civilizational, cultural or familial heritage, but the Party.

As developments compounded, the people of Hong Kong began to push back. 1997 increasingly came to be seen not as a 'return to the motherland' – a motherland, it should be added, that neither spoke our language, respected our values nor acknowledged our history – but as the replacement of one colonial power with another that is less tolerant, less liberal and even less accountable. Under the CCP, there was no opposition at all; only a Party that rewarded 'loyalty' with membership of the Chinese People's Political Consultative Conference (CPPCC) and punished non-compliance.

A number of approved democrats were invited to engage with Beijing, only for each to walk away when it became clear that 'consultation and dialogue' did not mean that Beijing was listening. Indeed, with Britain out of the way, the CCP consistently refused to allow the issue of constitutional reform to be tabled, let alone voted upon.

It's easy to see in retrospect that Hong Kong should have fought harder when the British were still at the table. Perhaps we could have used activism to help shape a more robust arrangement. Because the trouble with the Sino–British Joint Declaration is that there is no mechanism for enforcement. The Basic Law, Hong Kong's constitution, leaves the interpretation up to Beijing. Thus universal suffrage and democratic representation, which according to the Basic Law is the goal Hong Kong is meant to be working towards, was interpreted with 'Chinese characteristics'. Hong Kong would soon discover what this meant.

Feeling Freedom Erode

While this politically fraught handover was taking place, I was growing up as a pretty typical member of my generation. I spent much of my time navigating Hong Kong's highly competitive school system. I was not a particularly diligent student. I joined my debating society and would on occasion play football after school. Outside of this I had no extra-curricular activities. I enjoyed playing video games. I didn't see myself as political, nor did I follow local politics very closely. I never dreamt of being a politician or an activist, nor did I want to be. But life is often funny that way.

Coming from a humble background, I grew up feeling that politics was very far removed from my life. We knew what was happening in Hong Kong, and while I could see and feel changes going on around me, it was hard to relate them back to the political discourse on the TV and in newspapers. I now see that politics is something people engage with when they believe they have the power to change society.

Where I was raised, there wasn't much hope or feeling of agency. My parents both had to work very hard to earn a living. Their positions were never secure, and they were sometimes unemployed or forced to change jobs. Our finances were always tight and often unstable. We lived in government-subsidized public housing, and I had limited opportunities to see beyond our closed world. This made me naturally inward-looking.

For much of my childhood and into my adolescence I felt free to speak what was on my mind. I was able to access information that interested me, even if it was critical of the Chinese regime. Through Yahoo! and Google, on messaging apps like ICQ and social media like Facebook, my generation were connected to the world. We watched politicians criticize the government, not only in Hong Kong but abroad. We appreciated the value of criticism to hold power to account, and to make change for the better. We could listen to speeches and watch or read about peaceful protests. We were proud of the freedoms we enjoyed, and the fact that we lived in a city that had a proper justice system, even if life was not always fair.

This was markedly different to what we saw happening in China, where lawyers, journalists, labour and human rights activists were being jailed and corruption was endemic. You didn't have to be deeply interested in politics – the contrast was unmistakable.

In our way of life, in our governing structures, in the degree of freedoms we enjoyed, we understood how different Hong Kong and China were. Our two societies had taken divergent paths. Before ever learning about 'One Country, Two Systems', I instinctively understood what it meant in practice: that Hong Kong can only survive because of our differences to the Mainland. Our governing system allowed for Hong Kong to continue as a pluralistic and international society in a way that China could never be under a one-party dictatorship. Our system had much more in common with foreign liberal democracies like the US, the UK, Canada and Australia, with whom many Hong Kong people had ties. And, as in these countries at their best, Hong Kong celebrated and found strength in its openness and diversity, rather than a narrow conception of racial nationalism.

Yet for Beijing the emphasis was never on Two Systems but on the recognition of One Country: the Two Systems could only exist or be understood as part of One Country, under the control of One Party. Despite its legal obligations as the co-signatory of the Sino–British Joint Declaration, Beijing has now declared the treaty a 'historic document' to which China is not legally bound. For Beijing, Hong Kong is only a milestone in a nationalist narrative for the 'reunification' of China, a critical step in 'restoring' China to its rightful place as a leader among nations.

The feeling of living freely gradually began to disappear. The changes happening in Hong Kong were everywhere, perhaps especially among those most lacking a voice. I felt it, as did my family and friends. We saw it in small changes to our way of life, and to the way our language was being challenged. We saw it in a change in attitude: tourists who no longer respected Hong Kong's differences and who saw our home as just another city in China; shop staff who discriminated against local residents; in the tone and language of officials and those with authority. Most significantly, we felt this change in our understanding of our home, our identity and our history, and in what we were being told to remember.

For my generation, one of the watershed moments was in 2014, when the civil disobedience Umbrella Movement emerged. There was no aggression. People chanted slogans and sang songs, while across the city lines of police officers and riot police were being mobilized.

A friend of mine, who was observing the gathering crowds from an overhead footbridge, tells me he knew that day we were about to witness a clash between two competing ideas of Hong Kong – the first time these two versions of the city had come into open conflict. The first was led by a new generation that embraced the city no longer as immigrants but as native Hongkongers. This generation dared to be idealistic, and to imagine a new type of politics. Most of all, they did not fear China. The other was a Hong Kong authority that was in hock to Beijing.

As my friend watched the crowds go by, a line of policemen, fully kitted out to respond to a riot, marched past him. He greeted them but was violently pushed aside. As he fell to the floor, he looked up to see them shoving an elderly woman. On her face was an emotion rarely then associated with the Hong Kong Police: fear. 'I'd never seen the police so psyched,' he says. 'It was as if they had been conditioned not to react to the actual situation, but to see and respond to a situation that did not exist.' The Hong Kong Police, we would later discover, had been prepped by Chinese security.

Despite controlling the legislature, Beijing failed to pass the electoral reform it sought in 2014. The Bill required a two-thirds majority to pass in the legislature, and in an almost comical show of incompetence thirty-one pro-Beijing legislators missed the vote when they left the chamber to wait for the arrival of one of their colleagues.

'Uncle' Lau Wong-fat, their tardy octogenarian colleague, was also a notorious clan and alleged triad leader who has been implicated in a swathe of criminal activity. In 2011, in his only attempt at elected office, he failed to win a District Council seat. He was nevertheless appointed to the council by the Chief Executive and promptly elected chair by pro-Beijing loyalists.* 'Waiting for Uncle Lau' soon became a popular slogan.

Looking back at the last years of colonial administration, many are reminded not of the freedoms we lacked but the freedoms we had. These freedoms were understood and respected by those who administered and governed the city. It was clear what was meant by democracy, universal

---

* In Hong Kong a new standard is being introduced. All parties in the judicial system, according to the CCP, have to be 'loyalists'. In Beijing's definition, they have to prioritize the CCP over the people and their values.

suffrage, representative government and freedom of expression. I intuited this atmosphere when I was growing up in the early 2000s. We dreamt of a new China, integrated into the free world through trade but also a responsible and respected member of the international community.

Two decades of 'One Country, Two Systems' has shown that Beijing is not capable of accepting two systems. As in Tibet, where Deng first proposed the concept, its true meaning has been revealed. A one-party state cannot accept pluralistic politics, nor an open and pluralistic society. Freedom of expression continues to be protected by law, but in practice it is heavily eroded. How can we speak honestly when people feel afraid even to express their desire to live free?

This is the tragedy. For China, Hong Kong is just the latest chapter in a long tale of restored national glory. But for Hongkongers it is a place and a home, a people and a way of life. It is only with freedom that we will find the dignity to live as we are and not as Beijing imagines us to be.

My First 4 June
Candlelight Vigil Experience

My first experience of peaceful resistance was not in 2014, but three years earlier, when I attended the annual vigil to commemorate the Tiananmen Square Massacre. In order to understand why the tragic events of 4 June have become so symbolic for free Chinese people, we first have to examine why people had gathered in the square in the first place.

In 1989 China was rocked by mass protests. People, especially students, felt it was time for political reform. They did not oppose the CCP, but believed it needed to evolve with the country, loosen its control and allow for a more representative form of government. They dared to hope for a peaceful transition to a free society. Mass peaceful protests erupted in cities across the whole of China. But it was understandably in Beijing, the capital, where the focus lay.

On 4 June 1989, the People's Liberation Army, sworn to protect not the people but the Party, opened fire on peaceful protestors in Tiananmen Square. Tanks were unleashed against the flower of Beijing's universities. Thousands died simply for asking for change, simply because they dreamt of a better political system. Calls for democracy, for an end to corruption and an open government were met by bullets. The images were broadcast across the globe.[*]

In Hong Kong the impact of the Tiananmen Square Massacre was immense. The city ground to a halt as people tuned in to news reports. People cried on the street.

I first learnt about the 1989 protest when I was in secondary school. This was actually quite late, as many of my friends had already been told about it by their families. For those who came from freedom-loving homes, it was an important lesson in the nature of the Chinese regime and a key example of why the CCP cannot be trusted. However, my family was apolitical and I studied at schools run by pro-Beijing

---

[*] To find out more about the 4 June Tiananmen Square Massacre, including contemporary estimates of the death toll, see https://www.bbc.co.uk/news/world-asia-china-42465516; on how the CCP has revised this out of history, see Louisa Lim's *The People's Republic of Amnesia* (OUP, 2014).

organizations. We didn't talk about politics or about recent Chinese history at home, and at school the truth about 1989 was kept from us. Instead, I learnt about what happened from a group of friends, with whom I would later attend the vigil. My curiosity piqued, I did some research.

I was horrified by the accounts of journalists who witnessed what took place, and by the commentaries that followed. That the sincere demands of the dissidents were both so relatable and inspiring only made the crackdown all the more tragic.

I will always remember the first time I saw the videos of brave Chinese citizens protesting to their government that they wanted a say in how their country and lives were run. The Party was always talking about 'the people', and here they were. They demanded freedoms that were their due under their own constitution. I had never seen such hope and idealism in the eyes of Chinese people. To keep watching, to see all that was good and true crushed so brutally by bullets and tanks, hit me hard. Like so many others before me, I felt a deep betrayal. Had I not been denied the truth by my school, had I properly understood the freedoms we enjoyed in Hong Kong sooner, perhaps I would have felt this betrayal less keenly.

Learning about 4 June made me aware of how lucky I was to be in Hong Kong, and how much I had taken for granted. I had seen what happened when power was left unaccountable. To have a government of the people and for the people may be the ideal, but the bottom line is surely to have a government that is compelled to listen.

The vigil in memory of the 1989 Tiananmen Square

Massacre had taken place every year since 1989 in Hong Kong, and is one of the largest memorial events anywhere in the world. I was seventeen years old when I first went. Like many Hongkongers, attending the vigil represented a coming-of-age experience for me: I was old enough to know the truth and comprehend what it meant. Most of all it represented the beginning of my maturity – to feel for the suffering and the dashed hopes of the generation before mine. The vigil mattered not only to honour those who died, but also to remember. Memories matter. Hong Kong was free because we were allowed to remember, and therefore to know. In China, people and memories are silenced, and the truth rewritten.

That day I met my friend in Tung Chung on Lantau Island, where we both lived. We took the subway to Causeway Bay on the island of Hong Kong. It was the closest station to Victoria Park, where the rally is always held. The journey took an hour. All the trains heading to Causeway Bay were full to overflowing. Everyone was dressed in black. This sea of black mourning flowed across the city, crowding out buses and streets, as it made its way to the starting point. This river of bodies seemed itself to be a form of protest.

From within the station, we could hear the loudspeakers hailing protestors on the street. All along Great George Street, in the direction of the park, were stalls erected by local pro-democracy organizations and political parties. Well-known and much-respected public figures were there too, canvassing the crowd for support. My hands were soon filled with flyers and booklets. Some detailed the events we were remembering, with first-hand accounts and witness testimonies, while others outlined political manifestos promoting democracy in Hong Kong. I learnt from the materials that a student representative from Hong Kong was in Tiananmen Square in 1989 as the tanks entered, and that his life was saved by fellow protestors and the ordinary people of Beijing, who formed a human shield around him so he might escape. Knowing that their government would seek to hide the truth, these courageous people were prepared to risk their lives in the hope that the student representative might return with the truth to Hong Kong, from where it would reach the world. Reading this, I was in tears. That day I read every word on every leaflet, and my heart wept with every story. That day I learnt what it truly meant to feel solidarity, and to be a Hongkonger with a free spirit. It was my first education in politics and in the power of political activism.

As we reached the park, we were directed towards the football pitches. Here tens of thousands of people had already gathered. Many more were filing in. Volunteer ushers guided people in lines to keep order and to ensure that each pitch was completely filled. My friend and I followed, and were soon sat in our own little space. My friend explained to me that we needed candles and ran off into the crowd to find them. He soon returned with two. When it was time, we lit them and observed a silence as the memorial ceremony got under way. On that night, we remembered what the Chinese government and the rest of the country would not – a memory of hurt, grief and anger that CCP loyalists on the Mainland do not acknowledge, and the young increasingly do not know.

During the ceremony songs were sung and flowers passed

among the crowd. Many people wept as we watched video footage and heard from survivors. We felt the trauma of those who had given up so much to dare to believe in a better, free China. We remembered those who died, but also those who survived and who could now only speak to us as exiles.

'Release the dissidents! Rehabilitate the 1989 pro-democracy movement! Demand accountability for the 4 June massacre! End one-party dictatorship! Build a democratic China!'

This was the call. To me it seemed much more than a slogan. There was a poetic sense of justice about the words.

Who there on that day in 1989 could have imagined the CCP would crush the protests with such brutality even as the whole world was watching? Who would have thought the regime would so completely hide the truth from the country's children and grandchildren? And who among the hopeful crowds that day would have thought that Hong Kong, a city which so many on the Mainland once associated with openness and freedom, would later have to face its own crackdown under the auspices of the same ruling party?

There is now a dark shadow over the city I called home. No one knows what the red lines are any more. Facing the possibility of trial without a jury, by a judge selected by a Chief Executive accountable only to Beijing, and possible life imprisonment in a prison system that operates 'black jails' where people are held without trial, the risks have never been higher.

Freedom Measured in Opposition

Without freedom of speech, we cannot share the stories that lead us to the truth. When we cannot freely exchange ideas, the world we can imagine is limited to that which we can imagine alone. And, more practically, when we cannot speak freely it is harder to connect with and encourage like-minded people to stand together for positive change. When governments control access to information and are able to define the narrative and dictate what we know, we lose more than our freedoms. We lose the ability to see the world for what it is. We lose our humanity.

Only tyrants fear their own people. Only an illegitimate form of power fears criticism. Only a weak and insecure regime fears change.

When I call out to 'end one-party dictatorship', I feel in me an inherent power: the power to imagine and to hope that change is possible, and that I can be a driver of that change. It is a power we all possess. I feel the power we all have to shape the type of world we wish to live in. To be able to speak with sincerity of what I truly think, feel and believe is itself empowering. It is this power that authoritarian governments most fear and feel they must suppress.

If Hong Kong people were like people in Mainland China – if our access to information was curtailed and our government compelled us to accept, without criticism, only the official narrative – there would be no remembrance. We would, like so many people in China, no longer envisage being free. It would not mean the memory of the crackdowns would be wiped clean, but that those who remember would be forced to remain silent. The pain of a great injustice would be bottled up, unacknowledged, let alone addressed. It would mean a fundamentally unstable society, not the 'harmonious' society Beijing claims, but one where people are forced to suppress what they think because of the limits to what they can say. With some not knowing the truth, and others lacking the freedom to discuss what they know, we would live our lives without ever understanding each other. We would live in a society lacking in true empathy and compassion.

We are not just economic animals, and society is much more than just an economy. Free places provide refuge, as Hong Kong did to the many activists and dissidents who fled China following 1989. It was to Hong Kong that reporters came with secretly shot video footage that would have put their lives at risk in China. In Hong Kong this footage could be broadcast freely.

But Hong Kong is also a lesson in how authoritarian power undermines a free society. It may not always arrive in a tank. It does not always happen overnight, by means of a coup. More often than not, it happens through a million subtle adjustments, each in itself so incremental that it might seem unnecessary to object. It happens through the increasing presentation of political authority as unchallengeable and infallible, through the demonization of opposition figures and the delegitimization of dissent. It happens when governments no longer seek to manage the official narrative but to define reality. The authoritarian targets places and sources of learning: schools, the media, the internet. A free press is undermined not by a single diktat but by attrition. The rule of law ends not when lawyers are hanged from the scaffold as traitors, but when our understanding of the law itself is changed. It is a shift so subtle you might miss it, and then one day you realize that you have had a thought that you are afraid to say out loud.

Freedoms are lost by unjustifiable red lines, and more so by not knowing where the red lines are drawn. China's definition of what constitutes a threat to 'national security' is deliberately obscure. The result is a people who never know what exactly they are allowed to say or do – who live in constant fear that they may, unintentionally, cross the line, the punishment for which is severe and is not limited to yourself. The love we have for our family and loved ones is used to silence us. After a time, the regime hopes, society itself will change. This fear will become so embedded as to no longer be questioned. We lose our freedoms because we have forgotten what it was to be free.

A Free Press

Freedom of speech is recognized as a fundamental human right. Article 19 of the United Nations' Universal Declaration of Human Rights (UDHR), which China not only signed but helped to draft, incorporating elements of Confucianism, states:

> *Everyone has the right to freedom of opinion and expression; this right includes freedom to hold opinions without interference and to seek, receive and impart information and ideas through any media and regardless of frontiers.*

This freedom is reflected in, and is to a degree dependent on, a free press. It allows us to be openly critical, but also to appeal to public opinion to hold power to account. But not all news organizations are equal, or report to the same standard. We must consider not only preferences, which all media outlets will have, but whether they are making efforts to minimize biases, and also whether they have an agenda. Who owns or funds a paper, and what do they gain from it? Perhaps more importantly, who sets the tone and the editorial line?

Some of the best news reporting is done by independent state broadcasters. The British Broadcasting Corporation (BBC), the American Public Broadcasting Service (PBS), the Australian Broadcasting Corporation (ABC) and the Canadian Broadcasting Corporation (CBC) are rightly respected around the world. In Hong Kong there is Radio Television Hong Kong (RTHK), which was set up by the British and based on the model of the BBC. Despite receiving public money, all are editorially independent, and operate with a principled journalistic mission to report accurately and objectively, with high journalistic integrity. Unlike commercial broadcasters they are protected to a degree from the demands of the market, which may reward sensationalism over objectivity or public interest (and we should note that public interest means news that is in the interests of the public good, rather than simply stories the public might be curious about).

Independent state broadcasters are not to be confused with state-controlled broadcasters and newspapers, which are not operated independently and are used specifically to promote a national narrative. Broadcasters like Russia Today

(RT) and China Global Television Network (CGTN), and state-controlled papers like *China Daily* and *Global Times*, are political tools. They are not accountable to the truth, but to the political line of their respective regimes. They promote a line rather than investigate the truth. When we engage with such media we must remember that we are not being presented with a perspective but a political narrative that may diverge widely from reality.

Commercial media companies often receive much attention for adopting a partisan bias. In the US, Fox News and MSNBC are heavily criticized by those who do not share their political leanings. Americans are right to be critical, but remember that this is a luxury not available to those who live in societies lacking such freedoms. Commercial companies still have an obligation to report truthfully, and when they don't they can be challenged. Although there may be a commercial incentive to be sensational or even mislead, they cannot lie and their reporters are tied to respecting good practice. They will not, as CGTN has been found to have done, partake in arranging and broadcasting forced confessions,* or cross the line from presenting misleading information to running active campaigns of disinformation.†

In Hong Kong, our proud history of press freedom, despite being highly valued by society, has been eroded. The

---

* 'Chinese TV channel breached rules with "forced confession"', https://www.bbc.co.uk/news/entertainment-arts-53308057

† 'China Media Bulletin: CCTV spreads disinformation, Hong Kong journalists attacked, activists die in custody', https://freedomhouse.org/report/china-media-bulletin/2019/china-media-bulletin-cctv-spreads-disinformation-hong-kong

erosion has come from within, from a society whose relationship with the media is shifting due to a political narrative that
frames the free press as 'Western' and in opposition to the
'Chinese' perspective of state-controlled media. But there has
also been direct interference from China:

> *Hong Kong saw many cases of violence against the media,*
> *mainly by the police and pro-Beijing criminal gangs, during*
> *the pro-democracy demonstrations in the summer and*
> *autumn of 2019. The territory is supposed to enjoy separate*
> *status as a special administrative region of the PRC until*
> *2047, but press freedom is already in retreat as a result of*
> *pressure from Beijing. The most notable recent incident was*
> *the expulsion of Financial Times Asia editor Victor Mallet in*
> *October 2018. As vice-president of the Foreign*
> *Correspondents' Club of Hong Kong (FCCHK), Mallet had*
> *chaired an event that wasn't to Beijing's liking.*

This is an excerpt from Reporters Without Borders (RSF)
2020 press index report. Hong Kong had been eighteenth in
the world rankings for press freedom in 2002, but in its most
recent report the country has dropped to eightieth. This is a
spectacular plummet at a time of growing authoritarianism
and threats to press freedoms globally.

Reporters have been regularly attacked by the Hong Kong
Police and by pro-Beijing supporters, neither of whom are
held to account. Foreign journalists have been threatened for
simply doing their job. Victor Mallet's infraction was to host
a forum with a public figure disliked by the authorities. Mallet is not an activist. No law had been broken and he was

simply doing what journalists are supposed to do – listen to all sides of the story. And yet, after travelling to Bangkok two months later, he returned to find his work visa denied, and was questioned for four hours by immigration officials before being allowed to re-enter Hong Kong.

The environment in which the press must operate has become intensely hostile. The government portrays journalists as an enemy, and has stoked resentment within the community for independent and free-press outlets. The best in international journalism, from the BBC and Al Jazeera to the *New York Times*, are labelled as 'Western' and 'anti-China'. The most fact-checked news sources are declared purveyors of 'fake news'. The BBC, for a long time banned in China, but available in international hotels, was removed completely in early 2021. Hong Kong followed suit, banning it from public broadcast.* The *New York Times* has moved much of its key operation out of Hong Kong to Seoul, in South Korea, and other major international news agencies are similarly looking to relocate. Hong Kong, once Asia's most free city and a bastion of press freedoms, is no longer so.

When journalists are denied a safe environment in which to work, when they must consider the sensitivities of every situation and every person they meet for fear of dire repercussions to themselves or their sources, it becomes ever more dangerous to hold power to account. This changes the relationship we all have with power, and has heightened the

---

* 'Why China banned the BBC, and why it matters', https://www.cnbc .com/2021/02/16/china-blocks-bbc-world-news-after-uk-revokes-license- of-cgtn.html

problem of Hong Kong's democratic deficit and lack of political freedoms.

It is not only journalism that is changing, but the whole media landscape. Local media companies have gradually been bought out by pro-Beijing interests. A media that was once representative of the people is now another way of shaping the people. Independent journalism is not only targeted by political forces, it is increasingly being pushed to the fringes. Cable TV News, one of the most reputable news outlets in Hong Kong, was bought following its protest coverage and has been completely restructured, with a new leadership and a new editorial line.[*] Hong Kong's public broadcaster, Radio Television Hong Kong (RTHK), has undergone a similar shake-up.[†]

Many of Hong Kong's most experienced and well-respected producers, commentators and reporters have been laid off, despite there being no economic justification for such cost-cutting. Their replacements are either proponents of the government line or are too early in their careers to risk stepping out of line. Similarly, senior executives with a journalistic background are being replaced by bureaucrats such as Patrick Li at RTHK, who previously worked in the

---

[*] 'Beleaguered TV network i-Cable to be sold to new Hong Kong investors', https://hongkongfp.com/2017/04/21/beleaguered-tv-network-i-cable-sold-new-hong-kong-investors
'Lay-offs at Hong Kong TV station stoke new concerns over media freedom', https://www.reuters.com/article/hongkong-media-idUSKBN28B4BL

[†] 'Hong Kong signals overhaul of public broadcaster RTHK, stoking media freedom concerns', https://www.reuters.com/article/us-hongkong-security-media-idUSKBN2AJ09J

government's constitutional and Mainland affairs and security bureaus.

The Yuen Long attacks saw a mob of white-shirted village clansmen, armed with sticks and incited by a prominent pro-Beijing lawmaker, attack passengers who were returning home by train. The mob entered the train station and viciously attacked anyone they caught, including many commuters and even a pregnant woman. A journalist who began filming the mob was herself attacked. Her footage garnered worldwide attention. (The journalist, Gwyneth Ho, who was later disqualified from standing for election to the legislature, has been arrested under the National Security Law.*) Despite a flurry of desperate calls to the police, the same force that had been so quick in response to protests, often with violence, were slow to the scene. They then did nothing to stop the attacks and made no arrests on the site.

Bao Choy, a documentary producer in RTHK, and her team had painstakingly pieced together what happened that day through publicly available information. It did not seek to apportion blame but to establish the facts, which raised serious questions about the police. The mob were identified as being from nearby clan villages with deep connections to organized crime groups known as triads. Triads had since colonial times played a key role in Communist Party United Front efforts in Hong Kong. They were used as enforcers, and were closely tied to pro-Beijing associations.

---

* 'Notes from prison – how do I view my own stand?', https://chinadigitaltimes.net/2021/04/translation-notes-from-prison-how-do-i-view-my-own-stand-by-gwyneth-ho

The triads were also monitored by the police, who had a specialized unit based in Yuen Long to deal with triad activity. Not unreasonably, rumours quickly spread that the police had in fact been working with the triads on the night of the attack. It was the nightmare scenario envisioned by a young local filmmaker in the 2015 film *Ten Years*, which tapped directly into the growing sense in the community that Beijing had resurrected this old relationship.

Bao may have done the public a service in establishing the timeline of that day, but she was arrested and charged for improperly using publicly available information garnered from car license plate registrations. What she had done was common practice in investigative journalism, and in ordinary circumstances there would not have been a case. The message was clear: journalism should serve the government and avoid asking inconvenient questions.

Then, in June 2021, *Apple Daily*, the last openly pro-democracy mainstream newspaper in Hong Kong, closed. Eight of its directors were arrested under the National Security Law, including its founder, Jimmy Lai, and editor-in-chief Ryan Law. Its offices were raided twice in a matter of months, and on both occasions the raids were made a public spectacle. On the second occasion, 500 policemen were deployed. The company's bank accounts were frozen, and an attempt to hold a shareholders' meeting to decide what to do was broken up. Unable to pay its bills, its remaining board members, all of whom are no longer resident in Hong Kong, had no choice but to close it down.

We see our freedoms being eroded through such dramatic cases, but it is in the cumulative effect that we feel the loss.

We like to think of dictators and authoritarian regimes as almost ineptly brutal. But many are not. Leaders from Orbán in Hungary to Putin in Russia or Erdoğan in Turkey have dismantled free institutions and civil society gradually and steadily, piece by piece. They do not seek revolution, but rather to guide societies towards accepting their oppression. We lose our freedoms when we no longer truly believe in them, when being free no longer matters to us. The aim is not to oppress people, but for people to no longer be capable of recognizing their own oppression.

Dictators do not publicly embrace the authoritarian nature of their power. They cannot, as it lacks moral legitimacy. So they twist the words we have come to associate with universal values. The largest pro-Beijing, anti-democratic political party in Hong Kong is thus the 'Democratic' Alliance for the Betterment of Hong Kong (DAB). The 'National Security Law' is used to terrorize citizens. The rule of law is undermined by new 'understandings' sold to us as necessary to 'restore rule of law'. State-controlled propaganda markets itself as equivalent to free and independent news, presenting 'the other side of the story' – the slogan of Russia Today (RT), Russia's state-controlled broadcaster, is 'Question More'.

In Hong Kong the news will continue to be broadcast, and journalists continue to report. There will be criticism, but it will exist only within that space in which criticism is allowed to exist – in between boundaries Beijing shifts at will. The international press will need to balance truth with access, as they already do in the rest of China. In reality, Hong Kong no longer has a Fourth Estate.

Since 1982, freedom of speech has been enshrined in the Chinese constitution. Article 35 reads: 'Citizens of the PRC enjoy freedom of speech, of the press, of assembly, of association, of procession and of demonstration.' However, in reality this freedom, as with all others, has always been understood to be conditional. Free speech is a human right, yet rather than viewing human rights as something we all inherently possess, the CCP sees these 'rights' as serving the Party. Our right to freedom of expression is thus weighed against the two prevailing interests of the regime: to ensure stability and the conditions for economic development; and to maintain the Party's legitimacy in the eyes of its people. So, in Beijing's definition of free speech, 'You can say anything we want you to say.'

Living without Freedom

Many of my friends no longer use social media. Being of a generation that grew up with it, and that uses it regularly to see what's happening, access news and to connect with people, the decision to leave is not taken lightly. Yet it is a decision many have felt compelled to take.

I often read on Facebook comments from people who are annoyed that some of my more high-profile friends have left. I saw the number of my Facebook friends drop significantly as the National Security Law came into force; it fluctuates depending on the political situation. If this was happening because people no longer agreed with my politics, it would be understandable, if perhaps disappointing. I know friendships have been strained by Brexit in the UK or the partisan divide in the US. But, sadly, I think my friends are in a different situation. I know that many of those who can no longer publicly acknowledge their friendship with me do not think any less of me as a person or as a friend. I can no longer be connected to them as they are afraid they will be targeted by the state.

When you don't know what might constitute an offence, and when there is nobody who is independent of political power to defend your rights and hold that power to account, the only refuge is in silence. We self-censor not only what we dare do or say, but even those with whom we choose to associate. Relationships become brittle.

For me, and for many other dissidents and activists, the realization that many of our relationships are dictated not by the value we place in each other but by fear of political persecution hurts the heart as much as it does the head. It creates a sense of insecurity that tortures people. It's all too easy to suspect our friends or colleagues of betraying us – to see in our relationships not value, but risk. When people stop having faith in each other, the way we interact changes. The social fabric of our lives unwinds, and with it our ability to relate to one another.

A friend, another Hongkonger who is in exile in the UK, describes how those closest to him, his godfather and people he had once affectionately called his uncles, no longer wish to know him. Though he was born and raised in Hong Kong, and is as dedicated to Hong Kong as I am, his relationship with his home city is now not acknowledged by those to whom he was once close; the pain of having to leave his home is denied, and his moving to the UK is instead presented as a 'return home'. This is because my friend is not completely ethnically Chinese, but of mixed race. So, despite being from a family who have resided in and identified with Hong Kong for many generations, he does not belong – because Hong Kong does not belong to its people, but to Beijing and those it deems 'patriots'.

Identity and belonging begin with self-expression. As the Chinese essayist and intellectual Liu Xiaobo wrote:

> *Freedom of expression is the foundation of human rights, the source of humanity and the mother of truth.*

> *I have no enemies and no hatred. None of the police who monitored, arrested, and interrogated me, none of the prosecutors who indicted me, and none of the judges who judged me are my enemies.*

> *Hatred can rot away at a person's intelligence and conscience. Enemy mentality will poison the spirit of a nation, incite cruel mortal struggles, destroy a society's tolerance and humanity, and hinder a nation's progress toward freedom and democracy.*

I find these words very poignant, reflecting the writer's deep understanding of how oppression works. Hatred of an imaginary other, not love of the person, is what binds unfree societies.

Living without freedom is like being in a park where we might see the grass, admire it and thank the authorities for building us such a beautiful space, but we are never allowed to touch the grass and enjoy it for ourselves. It is all for show.

In Hong Kong the government established Civic Square by the legislative buildings as a space for people to protest. It was for entering Civic Square that the police arrested activists and students in 2014, triggering the Umbrella Movement and the peaceful occupation of much of the city.

All those student leaders who led the protest that day at Civic Square have now either been imprisoned or are in exile. Joshua Wong, jailed for his participation in the 2019 protests, now faces a charge of subversion under the National Security Law; viewed by Beijing as a 'leading troublemaker', it is likely he will grow old in prison. Dozens of other political campaigners, including the legal scholar Benny Tai, former student activist Lester Shum and former legislator and environmental activist Eddie Chu Hoi-dick, are also facing the same charges. The list of victims grows longer.

I left Hong Kong in June 2020. Not long afterwards, my name appeared on the Chinese state-controlled news agency claiming that I was a wanted fugitive and a secessionist who had been 'colluding with foreign forces'. Calling for Hong Kong people to have the right to decide their future does not make me a secessionist; and advocating that Beijing be held to its treaty obligations is not collusion. The CCP knows how much control it needs over the media to keep the truth twisted out of shape (by 2013 it was reported that over 2 million 'public sentiment analysts' were employed by Beijing to monitor public discourse). With a free press, people might find their voices once again.

Today Civic Square is a fortress of barricades and armed police, who patrol the area constantly. It is a heavy-handed metaphor for what has happened to Hong Kong's freedom. Designed as a space for peaceful protest, it is now strictly off-limits to the public.

If the fate of Civic Square and the 2019 protests symbolizes the fall of the Hong Kong I knew, the journeys Joshua and I have been through reflect the only decision left to make in this era of autocracy: do we stand firm for what we believe in and know to be true, or do we accept subjugation? In a free society, which Hong Kong was, we dared to dream that our future was ours to shape. It is a dream that united Joshua and me, and one that we shared with all of humanity who dare imagine life with freedom. It is why we must all, together, focus on the bigger picture and fight to defend our freedoms, no matter how imperfect, if they can still give us hope.

Protecting Our Freedoms

Freedom of expression is a core freedom on which other rights and freedoms depend. Society must be free to express the different perspectives that naturally exist, and that means valuing and protecting the Fourth Estate as much as we value and protect our personal freedoms. We must not take them for granted, nor be complacent in fighting to preserve them.

We must support independent and critical media of the highest journalistic standards, whether it be large and established names like the *New York Times* or Reuters, or small start-ups like Stand News in Hong Kong. We must recognize the threat posed by authoritarian regimes promoting state-controlled news which is unverified and unaccountable; and of propaganda mouthpieces being presented as an 'alternative' perspective.

Neither must we allow our language to be used in bad faith. Human rights and concepts like universal suffrage must not be redefined by authoritarianism, or given, as Beijing likes to say, 'Chinese characteristics'. These are not Chinese characteristics based on Asian values, but those of authoritarianism based on the political interests of the CCP.

Indeed, we must not confuse the CCP with being representative either of China or of Communism. China existed as a civilization for perhaps as long as 6,000 years, and as a single imperial state for 2,000 years. The PRC was founded in 1949, and the first thing it did was destroy that China. In the last seventy years, the Party has destroyed more of China's cultural heritage, killed more Chinese people and done more to ravage their souls than any foreign invader.

Neither is it Communist in the sense many people imagine – a universalist project aiming for equality and workers' rights. The PRC lacks many of the most basic welfare provisions, and is one of the most unequal societies: trade unions, like all civic bodies, are controlled by the state, and lawyers and labour rights activists are politically persecuted. Ethno-nationalism is encouraged and is central to the national psyche. China is 'Communist' only in so far as it is authoritarian and remains state-controlled.

We should not take for granted our own freedoms to engage with civil society and stand in defence of our values.

We must not allow our fixation with what is wrong in our own societies to blind us to the threat posed by genuinely authoritarian states who see our freedoms as an existential challenge. While it is healthy to be critical, we must avoid giving in to partisan divisions, which only open the door to those who seek to undermine the very essence of our freedoms.

Finally, how we choose to spend our money, whether through buying a product or investing in shares, has become a form of expression and a way of showing support for shared values.

The day after the raid on *Apple Daily*, the paper decided to print more copies. Five hundred thousand copies were printed for the 18 June edition, almost five times its usual circulation. In a show of support, many Hong Kong citizens waited overnight at newspaper stalls to ensure they could buy a copy. Even though people were threatened by the government and could not even guarantee that simply reading op-eds and commentaries in *Apple Daily* would not be an offence under the National Security Law, they still stood by the paper. Even though people knew that buying the paper would not change the situation, nor prevent the paper from closing, they still did it to send a signal. Many of those who bought the paper did not particularly like its tabloid style of reporting non-political news, yet understood that it represented much more than merely its content. What was at stake was a fundamental freedom and an institution that underpinned Hong Kong's values and way of life.

Believe in the power of people. Engage with people. Trust people; share your thoughts with them. Disagreement is fine. What is important is that we can have a dialogue and discuss openly and freely what is important to us. We cannot afford to be apathetic.

CHAPTER 3

RESISTANCE AND CIVIL SOCIETY

The first of March 2014 felt like an unusually hot day. The sun shone brightly. The cooler winter temperatures already seemed a long time ago as the sun's rays warmed my skin. It was on the inside, however, that I was really feeling the heat. It seemed to rise with my nerves. For the first time in my life, I was not simply the quiet boy at the back of the class.

A few months before, I had been elected chairperson of Lingnan University's student union. I had crossed a milestone and was about to take to the stage for the first time as the representative of a student body. It was the first step on my journey as an activist.

Lingnan University is a public-funded university in Tuen Mun, a satellite city in Hong Kong's New Territories district. It is a small university of only 2,800 students, and positions itself as Hong Kong's answer to a US-style Liberal Arts College, focusing on the arts, social sciences and business and vocational studies. However, this self-proclaimed mission has not turned it into an excellent teaching school, as the leadership of the school is still quite conservative and pro-government. The small campus and informal culture allow a close-knit community, both within the student body and between students and faculty.

Hong Kong is a hectic city, with a demanding and highly structured school system. Despite attempts at reform, much of the learning continues to be by rote. Chinese families prize education, not so much for its own sake as for the status it bestows. For those from poor families, like my own, a place at university was seen as a ticket out of poverty (though not as much as for previous generations). In a society lacking a universal pension scheme, it is a parent's investment in a child that will need to provide for them in old age. Children's lives are therefore lived, from an early age, with this goal in mind.

Going to university is often the first experience many young people have of living without family pressures. They have made it to the goal. Other pressures will follow, but for now they are allowed to be themselves – at least until the second year of study. At university there are new people to meet, from different backgrounds and with different perspectives. We are introduced to new ideas, learn to question what we know and thought. We find a space where we can confront and deconstruct questions that we have long struggled to answer, and ask new questions too.

University is a significant step in our mental and social development, not so much from what is taught in the classroom, but in the new freedoms we enjoy as we transition to adulthood. I took small steps. I was not one of those students who knew everyone in the department faculty or did lots of extracurricular activities. But, for the first time in my life, I did feel there were people I could really look up to, and who were kind and patient enough to mentor me. These few teachers gave me the confidence to address and think about questions that had long been on my mind. These questions often began from a deeply emotive place, but as I learnt to explore and contextualize them, I began to understand why I felt the way I did.

Why are the voices of Hong Kong people not respected by the Chinese government? Why did changes to Hong Kong society feel so instinctively dishonest, as well as wrong? Why did the official message that all Hong Kong's problems were merely down to economic and social issues, and an ignorance of China, feel so insulting? Everyone I knew seemed to be asking these same questions. Yet until now, very few of us had had the opportunity to discuss them so openly and to explore what they meant.

Beginning My Activism

I was elected to the union during my first year. I was studying for a degree in Cultural Studies. In Hong Kong, official involvement in student politics tends to be a first-year pursuit. From the second year onwards material considerations start to weigh more heavily: internships, graduation and getting that first job. Even though many students continue to engage as much as they can, they simply don't have the time to serve the union.

Like others, I shared these more material worries. I did not come from a family that could help me lay out a career path, nor support me during my studies. I worked part-time, taking on small jobs when I could, to pay for my living costs. Nevertheless, I knew deep down it was right to serve on the union. Hong Kong was reaching an inflection point that would shape its future.

I chose to run for the union because I believed I could represent the views of the overwhelming majority of students. I believed I understood what people were feeling, and wanted to work with others in trying to articulate it. I also believed the union might be a force for change, not only within the university but in society as a whole.

The questions everyone was quietly discussing about Hong Kong's future were important. Simply pretending that people didn't care, as the Hong Kong authorities did, either because of the ignorance (and arrogance) of the elite or because they were obliged to follow Beijing's official narrative, was not sustainable. Tempers had been simmering too long and were fast approaching boiling point under the stress of Hong Kong's underlying contradictions. How could a city be both free and open, and an integral part of an authoritarian state?

On the streets, Beijing's attempts to create a new and patriotic Chinese citizen had only fostered a growing sense of alienation. Making people choose between a sincere love for their city and an alternative Hong Kong defined by the CCP only resulted in the birth of Hong Kong's own nativist movement. The Hongkonger identity grew stronger (to distinguish ourselves from the 'Chinese' defined by the CCP) and resistance to Beijing's influence strengthened. The growing influence of Beijing in community life through community organizations, travel groups and welfare associations was becoming so pronounced as to challenge our sense of self.

What made the situation unbearable was that our government and those people who might act as a bridge between Hong Kong and Beijing were so disconnected. Inequality had increased significantly since 1997. The Hong Kong elites, increasingly shielded from reality, no longer felt checked by the need to maintain legitimacy through good governance. With Beijing the sole source of authority and arbiter of what was 'true', the elites busied themselves second-guessing Beijing's wishes, seeking to see what Beijing saw, rather than finding out for themselves what was happening in their city.

Between 1997 and 2014, Hong Kong had had three Chief Executives. All were elected by a committee over which Beijing has complete control. Two candidates from the pro-democracy camp had run – Albert Ho and Alan Leong, both respected lawyers and political moderates. Despite enjoying considerably more public support, they had no chance of winning. But by fielding candidates and running a campaign there would at least be a discussion, which would help Hong Kong society mature politically. The understandable presumption was that Beijing would keep its word on democratic elections. Democratic politics, after all, requires good faith.

The idea for the Occupy Central protests began in 2013 with an op-ed written by Professor Benny Tai entitled 'Civil disobedience is the most powerful weapon'. In the article, he suggested that an act of civil disobedience be conducted in the business and financial centre of Hong Kong should

Beijing refuse to honour its promise to implement genuine universal suffrage.* One of the aims of proposed sit-in protests was to raise what had been a local and Hong Kong–Chinese issue with Hong Kong's important business and international community, who had not only been apathetic to the concerns of ordinary Hongkongers but were also poorly informed. There was, sadly, a very noticeable difference between the level of discourse in the Chinese- and English-language press.

The idea of Occupy Central caught the imagination of many, especially students and younger people disillusioned by the failing status quo. Rather than simply seeking to engage in open-ended dialogue with local authorities and Beijing, for the first time it was suggested that engagement should come with specific demands. Though what was proposed was limited, the founders of Occupy Central believed that it could hurt Beijing badly. Bringing Hong Kong's political problems to the doorstep of the business elite would be a huge loss of face for Beijing and for the Hong Kong authorities. As one local commentator noted, and despite government fear-mongering, even if the disruption that ensued would not be significant, it would be far less than the city-wide shutdown caused each year by typhoons. For many people the idea of civil disobedience, and that through their own agency they might pressurize Beijing into honouring its promise, was inspiring. Rather than just attend pre-approved protest marches as in the past, Occupy Central suggested it was both

---

* '公民抗命的最大殺傷力武器', *Hong Kong Economic Journal*

right and just for us to break the law if necessary, albeit in a peaceful way, to stand up for our rights.

After planting the seed of civil disobedience, Occupy Central quickly gained momentum. Like many people of my generation who had been raised in an open and safe civil society and taught to venerate the law, the idea of crossing the line of legality was especially challenging. I was just a university student – I didn't see politics or activism as my future. Neither did my friends. The thought of having a criminal record frightened me. Would I be able to find a job? My family had struggled to put food on the table, and I could be their route out of poverty. How would having a criminal record affect my family's standing in their close-knit community? How would we be viewed by our neighbours, friends and the wider family? The conflict between doing right by my family and showing solidarity with my fellow citizens was one many in my generation struggled with. If there was one saving grace, it is that we did not struggle alone.

Occupy Central did not persuade a generation to rebel. It started a discourse around civil disobedience that led people to explore deeply held concerns in new ways. It inspired people of all ages and from many backgrounds, uniting teachers and students, professionals and the working class, to think carefully about what kind of society we wanted to live in. It opened the way to a deeper understanding of justice and its relationship with democracy and public accountability. It expanded what was possible. Many people began to realize that they were not subjects but citizens, and that the wilful rejection of the law is an act by which we can signal our refusal to accept the terms of an undemocratic, unaccountable and broken system.

The movement became the most united and powerful representation of civil society I have had the privilege to encounter. It was embraced by those groups who shaped the civic discourse – minority and labour rights groups, civic associations, professionals, lawyers and human rights groups, educators and intellectuals. Democracy may have been a common aspiration, but it is through civil society that our common values and aspirations are given form and can be acted upon. Civic institutions give people the means to form networks and access the resources, both material and intellectual, to mobilize and fight for their rights. Civil society does not open people's eyes to injustice, but is instead a sign that a society is already awake and engaged.

On 31 August 2014, Beijing published its long-awaited paper on electoral reform. The paper followed several months of selective consultation with people Beijing knew would say what it wanted to hear, making it a pointless exercise. In China this is called 'consultative democracy', even though we know it has nothing to do with democracy. The paper declared that Beijing would honour its promise of deciding the 2016 Legislative Council and 2017 Chief Executive elections by universal suffrage. Hong Kong people were entrusted with voting for their leader. The catch was that we could only vote for two or three candidates hand-picked by Beijing. The existing Election Committee, which Beijing controlled, had previously selected the Chief Executive. Now the same committee would select those who were allowed to stand.

It was pretty clear that choosing among pro-Beijing vetted candidates did not meet the definition of universal suffrage.

Organizing Class Boycotts

In reaction to the paper, my colleagues and I at the Hong Kong Federation of Students (HKFS) began to organize class boycotts in September. The election framework proposed had not come as a surprise. Our intention was not only to express the disappointment, anger and betrayal felt by the overwhelming majority of Hongkongers, but to 'boil up' sentiment in the lead-up to the proposed Occupy Central protest.

As the organizers had made clear from the beginning, the Occupy protest was meant to be a last resort. Some hesitated when the time came for us to act. I appreciate that to cross the line into breaking the law in the name of a higher ideal was one many people were struggling with. But I also knew it was at moments like this that we must find the courage of our convictions to do what was right.

Beijing knew full well that what it proposed was unacceptable – Hong Kong people had made their feelings clear in opinion poll after opinion poll. It could have appealed to public opinion by asking for understanding that this was the best it could offer now, given the political situation in China. Instead, Beijing insisted on presenting fake universal suffrage as the real deal, and the culmination of our democratic aspirations. It demanded not our understanding but rather our gratitude for meeting the 'aspirations of the Hong Kong people'. It couched betrayal in the language of liberation.

At the HKFS we understood that we were fortunate not to be burdened by the responsibilities that come later in life, and to be able to speak up freely and act in the name of an ideal.

Our actions and demand for democracy might further awaken public consciousness and inspire others who were more hesitant to do likewise.

The theme of the class boycott was 'Boycott Classes, Continue Learning'. The HKFS designed a five-day-long series of lectures to educate students while they were away from campus. We had reserved Tamar Park, a large open space near the Central Government Complex, as a rallying point. The organization involved was intense and could only be achieved with the help of an army of volunteers. One of the most difficult tasks we faced was to recruit enough volunteer teachers qualified and competent enough to devise a suitably rigorous curriculum. This could only be done with the dedicated support of educators and the academic community.

The response demonstrated the vitality of civil society. People of great ability and from many different backgrounds responded to the call. Respected professionals joined academics, educators and researchers at our makeshift campus to design and then contribute to our efforts. A group of professors and teachers formed 'Teachers in Solidarity with Student Strike' to organize teaching. Three speaking sites were established in the park, each providing seven seminar sessions each day over the four days of protest. In total, over 100 such classes were delivered on a variety of subjects, from those on the school's curriculum to others dedicated to new skill sets and ideas. In the words of the group's social media page:

> We are a group of college teachers calling upon teachers
> (from professors to teaching assistants with teaching

experience) to volunteer to teach during the student boycott. There will be diverse forms of open classes, workshops and activities at the site of the rally to assist students and citizens to learn and reflect about the difficulties and political impasses Hong Kong is facing today, and the importance and limitations of democracy and universal suffrage in solving our social contradictions. We need to use the limited freedom and space we still have to collectively brainstorm about the future of Hong Kong, and to expand our ability to imagine what can still be done to make the necessary changes for democracy and social reform to continue.

The essence of the events was to turn a negative symbol (skipping classes) into a productive and politically powerful one. We wanted the world to know that we couldn't be written off as lazy students looking for a week's holiday. Boycotting class was a means of protest, but also a process to learn and improve. It was also important to show that education is not confined to the classroom – it can happen anywhere. What matters is not the place, but what is being taught.

It was a huge success, with each session of classes attracting large audiences. We couldn't have been further from the picture of a disorderly and rebellious mob that the authorities attempted to paint. The reality of the protest to those who saw it only earned the movement greater respect. The protest was a magnet not only for ever-increasing numbers of students, but also for ordinary citizens who felt strongly that what we stood for mattered. This was civil society in action.

I was fortunate enough to find the time to attend several of those sessions I found most appealing. I listened intently to speakers with real authority discuss concepts around democracy and civil resistance from the perspective of their own professions. Some talked about the relationship between civic space and protest, while others explained the drive towards resistance in human psychology. Some talked about how political systems affect wealth distribution. It takes a mature and open society to entertain such public dialogue and discussion. Like many people who were there, I felt deeply proud of this display of Hong Kong at its best – a vibrant, peaceful and open society flowering within a closed and increasingly authoritarian system.

This was the society I wanted to live in. The tragedy of Hong Kong is that this very tolerance and freedom was deemed the greatest threat to authoritarian rule.

The Enemies of Dictators

Free citizens threaten an unjust social order. Free thought threatens national and political ideology. Civil society so threatens the CCP that Xi Jinping has declared it an enemy of China. It is sobering to think that many of those smiling students are being persecuted today, and that young Hongkongers coming up through the education system are now compelled to undergo 'national and patriotic education'. Of those speakers who inspired me then, some have been removed from teaching, others have left Hong Kong, and others now dare not even 'like' a Facebook post. This, according to the CCP, is 'correct thinking'; this is its harmonious society.

In the dictionary of dictatorship, civil society is the most important enemy to destroy, because it challenges their demand for complete control. It creates a new source of power outside of government, and a new source of legitimacy through solidarity with the people. Civil society is bottom-up, not top-down – it derives its meaning and value from the lived experience of people, whereas in a dictatorship values are imposed on people by diktat.

Civil society should engage with the public and private sectors, but it's important that it is able to operate outside the framework of both. Civil society is inherently independent. Civil society actors, such as NGOs and professional groups, will work with the government on different issues, but are not beholden to authority. They can and will oppose authorities if necessary. They are guided not by what the authorities decide is right and wrong, but by finding out and representing the concerns of society.

Dictatorships centralize power. They do so because they have to: when an opposition is anathema to your system, all power must be monopolized. This power always ultimately depends on military force. In 2019, China spent $216 billion on domestic public security, including state security, police, domestic surveillance and armed civil militia; this is more than it spends on the People's Liberation Army (PLA), China's formal military, which must swear allegiance not to the nation but to the CCP. Soldiers spend up to a third of their time studying Xi Jinping's approved brand of Communist ideology. But if force underpins dictatorships, it is through social control that authoritarianism is exercised.

Civil society is a challenge to this control. It challenges the legitimacy of the regime in the eyes of the ordinary people because it is better placed to speak on societal issues. This is because civil society actors arise from within the community itself. So in a democratic system, where legitimacy is reliant on the mandate of the people, and where governance is accountable, civil society is encouraged and valued. Indeed, it's seen as a sign of a healthy society, and a manifestation of the public's conscience. Authoritarians don't want to hear from a public that might contradict them, so civil society is often conveniently framed as an 'outside' conspiracy by hostile foreigners to undermine the authority and power of the regime.

In 2013, Communiqué Number 9, an official document about ideological censorship, was circulated among high-level CCP officials. The document outlined the CCP's 'seven unspeakable concepts' (七不講), being: universal values; press freedom; civil society; civil rights; the Party's historical errors; the 'crony bourgeoisie'; and judicial independence.* These are not allowed to be discussed in public. The Party was quite explicit that civil society has the capacity to establish political forces independent of the CCP. It is sometimes said that what the CCP objects to is politics, yet the CCP defines politics as any action that threatens their complete dominance, even unintentionally. The issue the CCP has with civil society is not that some civil society groups advocate around politically sensitive issues, but that civil society *by definition* is independent of political control.

---

* 'Xi Jinping's New Deal: There are 16 more points after seven', https://www
  .bbc.com/zhongwen/trad/china/2013/05/130528_china_thought_control_
  youth

Take the case of He Wei-jun. In 2007 He founded an NGO in Guangzhou in southern China to educate workers about labour rights and to help agricultural workers defend their rights. This wasn't about changing the law – it was simply about helping people to understand the laws that were in place. What motivated him was a sense of injustice, and a need to defuse growing tension within the community. He soon discovered that many of the injustices people faced suggested an institutionalized problem. Despite their rights under law, people were being left uncompensated after being injured at work; and the children of migrant workers were not entitled to an education. He himself was also a victim. In 2006, his hand was smashed by a heavy machine due to the fatigue he was experiencing after working for more than 24 hours without rest. He lost three fingers in this industrial accident, and with them the dream of establishing his own business. Yet his employer refused to compensate him and argued that it was his carelessness that had caused the accident. He fought the case at court after studying the labour law and won. Nonetheless, not everyone could achieve the same outcome. Seeing people repeatedly suffer from a systemic problem that could easily be fixed, he saw that the only way to address the issue was to advocate for change.

His NGO transitioned from providing services to focusing on raising awareness. But in 2014 the government's position on civil society organizations shifted; the limited assistance it had provided was cut. In 2015, his NGO was outlawed. He was arrested on a charge of embezzlement and jailed for 127 days. He had not challenged CCP rules, nor was he motivated to do so. What he cared about were labour rights. However, to Beijing what mattered was that his work had exposed an injustice in the system which might have provoked controversy and undermined the regime's control. No attempt was made to address the injustices themselves: these could be covered up.

An NGO is non-governmental for a reason: to be able to hold government to account. The whole purpose of an NGO is to seek a resolution to problems in society when systems don't work the way they should. All systems made by humans go wrong sometimes, since none of us are perfect. The important thing is that we are able to fix problems when they arise. The problem is that in a dictatorial regime, only the regime can demand change. To suggest that a government system is anything less than perfect is to be politically disloyal and to invite political turmoil.

Since Xi Jinping assumed power in 2012, the already limited civil space tolerated by the CCP has been heavily curtailed. Determined to turn back the clock towards a more centralized and ideological regime, Xi has cracked down hard on civil society. Issues such as workers' rights, once the spring from which Communism sprang, are today addressed in the manner of fascism – by closing down the space in which people can be heard. Xi has pioneered a technological totalitarianism that controls what people in China see, hear and say, and where only Party-approved reality and narratives can exist. Long before the election of Donald Trump as US president heralded a more hawkish attitude towards foreign affairs, Xi was leading China, which had never left the Cold War narrative behind, deeper into this mindset.

Civil society was once seen as universal, a common good

that transcended politics. With its loss we have left behind one of the key drivers of global progress – and one of our greatest safety nets when we are facing an unanticipated catastrophe.

Silence Kills

In January 2020, the first cases of a new illness, COVID-19, were detected in Hong Kong. There were heated discussions as to whether the city should close its border with China. People were extremely worried, and for good reason.

The virus which causes COVID-19 is known as SARS-CoV-2. It is most closely related to the original SARS virus (SARS-CoV-1), which first appeared in China in 2002, from where it spread into Hong Kong, where 1,755 people were infected and 299 people died. Outside China, these were the worst figures recorded globally, and Hong Kong was the city most affected. In this earlier epidemic, the Chinese authorities had again suppressed information, denying that there was even an outbreak until the new virus was detected in Hong Kong among people who had recently travelled to China. Far from taking control of the situation and working with the WHO and global community in an open and transparent manner, the CCP's instinct was to save face by seeking to cover up what happened. As it would do again in late 2019 and early 2020 when COVID-19 was first detected in Wuhan, China.

In 2020, the opinion of the majority of civil society actors, including leading doctors and health care professionals, was that the Hong Kong government should close the border and curb any possible inflow of virus carriers. In response the government held a press conference on 31 January, during which Chief Executive Carrie Lam stressed that she would not impose what she described as 'discriminative' measures and appealed to the public for an inclusive and mutually respected public health policy.* At the time, more than sixty countries had already closed their borders to Chinese nationals – countries that are today hailed as having coped best with what would become a pandemic. What was odd, and in contrast to the Hong Kong most of us remember, was the language and tone of the government.

On 3 February, the medical workers' union held a strike.† Lam responded by declaring that 'anyone who uses "extreme measures" to coerce the government is doomed to fail'. Beijing's reaction was also severe: *Ta Kung Pao*, a state-controlled paper, declared the act of striking to be 'soft terrorism'; and CCP-controlled labour unions and the United Front, a network of unofficial bodies that the CCP directs and uses to extend its influence where it might otherwise be sensitive, were mobilized to counter any dissent.

---

* 'Coronavirus: Hong Kong leader Carrie Lam says total border shutdown with mainland China discriminatory, but will ramp up quarantine measures', https://www.scmp.com/news/hong-kong/politics/article/3048419/hong-kong-leader-carrie-lam-urges-local-residents-not

† 'Wuhan pneumonia: the polarized reaction caused by the escalating strike of Hong Kong medical staff and forcing the government to "close customs"', https://www.bbc.com/zhongwen/simp/chinese-news-51368990

But why were Beijing and the Hong Kong government so hostile to common-sense recommendations from civil society? One of the reasons could be the background of the medical workers' union, which was founded during the 2019 protests and represented some outspoken activists. More revealing, perhaps, is that the authorities did not limit their contempt to this group alone but painted any opposition, even from moderate voices within the medical sector who were not politically affiliated, with the same brush.

Power is more than the ability to make decisions: the ability to determine what is right and wrong is an equally valid demonstration of power. When we are young, we listen to whatever our parents tell us. What they say is right, and there is no room for objection. When I was told that watching television is bad, and that I had to go to bed, I accepted this. I might have whined and grumbled about it, but power determined the outcome. My mother would switch the television off. Now imagine if some learned gentleman had knocked on the door and informed my mother that TV can help children learn about the world. Knowing my mother, she would have picked up the broom and shooed him out of the house. 'Get out! I don't need you to teach me how to raise my son!'

Behind this power there is also an insecurity. The tone is raised not because what the more learned person has said is wrong, but because it is not. It's not about the merits of the advice, but the challenge to authority. The same might be said of the way in which the Hong Kong government responded to the medical community's legitimate concerns. It was not the advice that warranted such a hostile response, but the act of civil society daring to raise its voice.

This extreme sensitivity and hostile attitude are a hallmark of the Chinese regime. Although it is unable to change facts, as it is on the ground in the Mainland, the CCP greets any criticism of China with howls of abuse. It is more than undiplomatic; it's insulting and often verges on the absurd. For having the temerity to call for an inquiry into the origins of a global pandemic, and for deciding against allowing a Chinese company to build its critical infrastructure – the thought of which would not even be entertained if the roles were reversed – Australia is debased as a nation. Australians are presented as uncivilized and racist, and the country has been described as gum stuck on China's shoe. Despite its own aggression, China labels Australia and the West in general as the aggressors who, it claims, are breaking with the accepted norms of international behaviour.

For a dictatorship, everything is about survival. There is no mechanism for a change in government, only the status quo or revolution. Everything becomes about power. To challenge the decisions of government is more than an irritation; it is a threat. The central authority is and must always be superior to the rest of society. This applies equally to specialist professions like medicine. If the government position differs from professional advice, people would suspect it of having an agenda, undermining trust.

The Hong Kong government never provided a convincing reason why a complete border closure with China was unfeasible. From a public health policy perspective, it is common sense that many countries closed their borders to pandemic hotspots. When these hotspots were no longer China, the Hong Kong government was quick to act and slow to lift restrictions.

The Hong Kong government's tone was inappropriate and its policy approach has been inconsistent; both seem politically driven. This erodes public trust. It is probably unsurprising, then, that although Hong Kong is one of the most educated cities in the world, it has one of the lowest vaccine take-up rates. The issue is not lack of confidence in the vaccines, but distrust of the government.

The treatment of Doctor Li Wenliang in China is a signal lesson in the disastrous outcomes of a weak civil society. Doctor Li died at the age of thirty-four due to a COVID-19 infection, and he was hailed a national hero afterwards. But before he was made a martyr by the Party, he was summoned to the police station and accused of 'making false comments' that had 'severely disturbed the social order'.

His crime had been to post a warning on social media about a new coronavirus outbreak in late December 2019, when the world knew nothing about this COVID-19 pandemic. The action of simply and honestly laying out what he saw at the medical front line turned him into a 'whistle-blower', a description he had never associated with himself. The government tried to silence him when he raised the first warning. His warning was quashed and ignored. China missed its chance to contain the virus – either because they do not believe in their people, or because they aren't prepared to listen to what the people say.

The consequence of this negligence was enormous. Without civil society, people cannot speak out. They lack the right to engage in meaningful discussion about matters of public interest and point out when things are going wrong. When no one is able to address the cracks that naturally form in any society, honest and hard-working people suffer. The death of Doctor Li might have been avoided, and the rapid spread of the pandemic lessened, if the government had worked with civil society to make sure people's warnings could be heard. Sadly, this was not the case in President Xi's China.

Taming Civil Society

According to the CCP, there are three ways to disarm the threat posed by civil society: by quashing it, taming it or neutralizing it – that is, either to destroy civil society, co-opt it to serve your interests or to render it silent and powerless, maintaining its facade while gutting it of meaning.

For civil society groups with a professional background, the authorities either encourage, or in some cases legally compel, such groups to co-operate with the government, building a relationship of dependence. In China, NGOs doing social work are recruited to work at the community level and incorporated into the system by providing government-supported social welfare assistance. Once dependent on government-funded projects, civil society groups lose the ability to act independently or to challenge the government when it is at fault. NGOs are therefore unable to develop their own values and ethics, because whenever they depart from the Party line they are immediately dismissed. In this way, civil society is effectively co-opted by the state and tamed.

The impact of the civil society groups can also be neutralized by creating a fake alternative. Generally speaking, Hong Kong has two streams of trade unions: those aligned with the pro-democracy Hong Kong Confederation of Trade Unions (HKCTU), and those aligned with the pro-CCP Federation of Trade Unions (HKFTU). The HKFTU was founded in 1948, when Hong Kong was still a British colony and most Hong Kong–Chinese workers were migratory. At the time there was little democratic consciousness, the political division mirroring the civil war being waged in China between two competing authoritarian systems, Communist and Nationalist. As the older organization, the HKFTU is larger and much better resourced, with 410,000 members in 251 affiliates and associated unions. A satellite organization of the CCP, the HKFTU assigns members to the Hong Kong legislature and executive, and is represented in China's National People's Congress (NPC). In contrast, the HKCTU was only established in 1990, emerging from a Church-sponsored labour organization with strong links to grass-roots labour movements. Through participation in rallies and collaboration with different political entities, the HKCTU openly declares democracy to be one of its guiding principles. It has a membership of 160,000 from sixty-one affiliated unions, and since 2016 has had no members in the legislature. It does, however, have a strong reputation among the public as an independent and progressive union that puts the interests of its members first.

Whenever there are controversies over labour rights or social welfare, both groups claim to be the 'worker's representative'. Although, as trade unions, they claim to represent similar interests, their attitudes towards certain labour rights could not be more different. Before the handover in 1997, the Provisional Hong Kong Legislative Council, Beijing's shadow legislature, tabled a motion to abolish several Bills which included the right to collective bargaining, a core tenet of trade unionism that authorizes a legally binding negotiation on issues including salary and work hours. And yet the pro-Beijing HKFTU voted in favour of the motion, which paved the way for the abolition of the right.*

While the HKFTU has understandably been heavily criticized, it is nevertheless able to dilute the support and legitimacy of the HKCTU, which operates as an actual grass-roots union. When the government needs to introduce a controversial policy, such as the National Security Law, being able to claim the support of the HKFTU allows the government to claim that it has the support of workers. This undermines the efforts of other civil society groups to speak up on the issue. And with the support of the government, the HKFTU has been able to expand much faster and maintain a high membership, which would suggest to those unaware of the context that the HKFTU is more representative of workers.

As the space in which civil society can operate continues to shrink, the ability to effect change is diminished and the government is freed to act in ways that benefit the powerful at the expense of ordinary people.

---

* 'How Hong Kong's Right to Collective Bargaining Is Still Dead', https://www.sbs.com.au/chinese/cantonese/zh-hant/audio/news-encyclopedia-how-hk-s-collective-bargaining-right-was-abolished

When Political Prophecy Becomes Reality

The annual Hong Kong Film Awards (HKFA) celebrates the best in the Chinese and regional film industry. Founded in 1982, the award ceremony for the 'Chinese Oscars' is broadcast every year across the Chinese-speaking world. But in 2016 the Chinese government banned it in China because of the Hong Kong film *Ten Years*.

Ten Years was commissioned and produced in 2015. Five up-and-coming Hong Kong directors were asked to imagine what their home would be like in ten years' time. On a budget of only HK$500,000 ($63,000), five short stories were shot independently. The producers did not know, nor did they have any say about, what these stories would be. The five short films they received were revealing.

Every one painted a picture of a darkly sinister, almost Orwellian city: a city where truth has become so precious that a young couple slowly went around cataloguing and then literally preserving (in glass jars) everything about their lives, before making the ultimate sacrifice and preserving their own (dead) bodies; where the authorities collude with gangsters to assassinate a pro-CCP official as a 'false flag' attack in order to justify a crackdown on voices of dissent; where people self-immolate outside the British Consulate, so desperate are they for the international community to speak out; where children are encouraged to hate local culture; and where a Cantonese-speaking father can no longer talk to his Putonghua-speaking son.

The five short films were presented as a single theatrical

release. No commercial cinema chain in Hong Kong would show such thought-provoking content. It was released only at a few art-house venues. Despite this – and despite the low budget and lack of advertising – the film was a word-of-mouth sensation. Arguably, no film in Hong Kong history has had the same impact. What people saw resonated very deeply. People wept openly while watching the film.

Ten Years was deemed by Beijing unacceptable and 'politically incorrect'. The Hong Kong political and film establishment, who are reliant on the China market, sought first to ignore it. When this became impossible they sought to play it down. Popular support was soon matched by enough critical acclaim for the film to be nominated for awards.

The suppression of *Ten Years* only made the film seem more prophetic. It vividly reflected the fears of Hong Kong people – that sense that they were losing their freedoms, local culture, their memories and connection with truth. The underlying message – of each of the stories, of the project and in the audience response – was that people did not trust Beijing or the local government to act in their interest. Each story put the interests of the Party above those of the people and of the truth. It was, without directly saying so, a searing indictment of authoritarian rule.

The film also reflects the hopelessness of the situation. None of the stories end happily. Several show release only in death. Death represents an escape from a reality that is increasingly unbearable, not because any of the protagonists experience physical pain but because of the psychological torment of having to live in a reality increasingly defined by lies. 'A place where there are lies everywhere,' was how Chloé

Zhao, who won the 2021 Best Director Oscar for *Nomadland*, described China. 'You felt like you were never going to be able to get out.' For Hong Kong people, what resonated so strongly in *Ten Years* was the feeling of slowly slipping into an alternative reality from which they might never escape.

It is not surprising that Beijing blacklisted the film. All mention of it was scrubbed from existence on the Mainland. To hear them tell it, Hong Kong people are grateful to the CCP for liberating them from colonial oppression. Only 'foreign pawns' like myself, who they claim must be supported and paid by evil foreign powers to undermine China, incite dissent. Beijing and the Hong Kong authorities cannot learn from the film because they cannot be allowed to even conceive of the problem.

In free societies, even ones without a functioning democratic voting system as Hong Kong once was, good governance demands that we deal in reality. Following the Communist-inspired 1967 riots, during which several people were killed and a bombing campaign terrorized Hong Kong, the colonial government responded by implementing a series of wide-ranging social and welfare reforms. Corruption was tackled. Amnesty and reconciliation were prioritized over vindication and persecution. The British looked at themselves, acknowledged their shortcomings, asked what they could do better, and changed. Even when the change is imperfect, even when our systems are flawed, in free societies we recognize that we must confront reality and seek to address issues as they are.

Under an authoritarian system, everything must conform to and serve an official reality. Culture and the arts, which by definition are meant to be an expression of new ideas, are debased as propaganda. Thus the art of China's most critically acclaimed and celebrated artist, Ai Weiwei, cannot be shown in the country of his birth. His work is being removed from display in Hong Kong too. The world the CCP is determined to build is not Chinese, but simply authoritarian. Just as the Nazis could not define what was German, neither can any political party do the same today. Our culture, values and identity are defined by the people.

A state-run newspaper described *Ten Years* as a 'virus'. 'In the eyes of Mainlanders, this movie is completely ridiculous, the scenes depicted in *Ten Years* will not happen in Hong Kong,' the article said. Nonetheless, *Ten Years* was voted Best Picture at the 35th Hong Kong Film Awards. As the winner was read out, the celebrity audience fell silent for a moment before a few dared an anxious clap. The whole spectacle was surreal and frightening. This was China's 'free' and 'open' city.

In China, all mentions of the awards ceremony, a fixture on the Chinese calendar, were erased behind the Great Firewall. There was no live streaming, no simultaneous news reporting, and no discussions. Somewhere in Beijing, the great spider of officialdom was spinning a new web of lies with which the CCP would ensnare the Chinese people. *Ten Years* became taboo.

Five years later, in 2021, the Academy Awards Ceremony, known as the Oscars, was not broadcast in Hong Kong. A spokesperson for Television Broadcasts Limited (TVB) described it as 'purely a commercial decision'. Nominated for Best Documentary Feature is the short film *Do Not Split*, which documents the 2019 pro-democracy protests from the protestors' perspective. It shows protestors to be idealists, not anarchists, and as locals with local grievances. They are peaceful people pushed to the brink by a violent and unaccountable government. They are not terrorists – a truth that many people who engaged with the protests remember.

As I watched the Hong Kong Film Awards, I could not help but wonder whether this would be the future of Cannes, the BAFTAs or the Academy Awards. Richard Gere, Brad Pitt, Lady Gaga, BTS, Elton John and Justin Bieber are just some of the artists already banned in China; all have been penalized for speaking with honesty about their concerns.

According to PEN America, it would now be impossible to make a film like *Seven Years in Tibet* (1997) about China's 1950 invasion of that country. It is already inconceivable for a Hollywood production house to make a movie that casts the Communist Party's rule in China in a negative light, or presents a view of history that does not conform to its narrative. In 2021 John Cena, the wrestler turned actor, and star of the *Fast and the Furious* franchise, apologized profusely to China and to the Chinese people for having once referred to Taiwan as a country. 'I'm sorry for my mistake,' he said. 'I must say now, it's very, very, very, very important that I love, and respect even more, China and the Chinese people.' Must a love and respect for China mean the denial of Taiwan and the denigration of Taiwanese people?

Civil society thrives because every member can speak out and truly represent themselves through art and other forms. If this avenue is closed, the vitality of a civil society is compromised and the circulation of ideas is curtailed. We must not let our arts be defined by Beijing. By accepting Beijing's intimidation, as we have, its demands and expectations only grow. Should one day the big names in our own award ceremonies need to pause and think hard before they dare to clap, it would be the utmost insult to the free spirit of artistic expression.

CHAPTER 4

RULE BY LAW

A free society is one in which power serves to protect our freedoms. For freedom to mean anything at all it must not only be guaranteed by law, but the law itself must be independent of political power and empowered to hold politics to account. We must use our freedom to reinforce freedom.

According to the World Justice Project, the rule of law is a durable system of laws, institutions, norms and community commitment that delivers on four universal principles:

1. Accountability: the government as well as private actors are accountable under the law.
2. Just law: the law is clear, publicized and stable and is applied evenly. It ensures human rights as well as contract and property rights.
3. Open government: the processes by which the law is adopted, administered, adjudicated and enforced are accessible, fair and efficient.

4. Accessible and impartial justice: justice is delivered timely by competent, ethical and independent representatives and neutrals who are accessible, have adequate resources and reflect the make-up of the communities they serve.

Courts must be allowed to act independently, without fear or favour. But the rule of law is not just about having a legal and judicial system, nor even how efficiently these systems work. It's about knowing why we have laws in the first place, and whom and what they are supposed to protect. The law must serve not the powerful but the people: it must provide security to all, equally and without favour. It must be guided not by a desire to enforce but to protect. It must be consistent, fair and, through the legislature, accountable to the people.

Justice is the soul of the law. In a society governed by the rule of law, it is justice, not force, that underpins the social contract. It is because people believe in justice, and believe that justice is possible, that people agree to obey the law. Of course, all around the world courts are underfunded, bureaucracy bogs down the process, and laws intended to work for justice may have unintended consequences. However, there is still a fundamental difference between an imperfect or inefficient system, where the wheels of justice may turn slowly, and a system where the law is not empowered to serve justice.

As the rule of law is ostensibly apolitical, it is possible for it to operate within an undemocratic political system, provided that system honours, understands and operates within the spirit of the law. Yet this situation makes the rule of law vulnerable to the influence of malign political force once the institutional intention to uphold the legal system disappears. This fragility manifests itself in the case of Hong Kong. Though denied political freedom, colonial Hong Kong was nevertheless administered by those to whom the rule of law mattered. The rule of law not only shaped Hong Kong society, creating a polity that was law-abiding and trusting of the authorities, it also helped provide a degree of political legitimacy. Hong Kong thrived and became a hub for business because people could have confidence that they would not have their possessions or liberty taken from them arbitrarily, and that anyone accused of wrongdoing could expect a fair trial.

The continuance of the rule of law following Hong Kong's handover to the PRC in 1997 was meant to provide surety, in law, that the rights and freedoms Hong Kong had enjoyed would continue, and set limits to the exercise of political power (which remained undemocratic and unrepresentative). This was especially important in reassuring Hong Kong's flourishing business culture, but also for its people, many of whom had only recently fled China and were all too aware that the rule of law does not exist there.

Being Elected a Legislator

There were seventy seats in the 2016 Legislative Council (known to Hongkongers as Legco), before the election overhaul in 2021. Half of these were elected by the public through 'geographical' constituencies. The remaining seats were elected by interest groups through 'functional' constituencies, the majority of which were effectively controlled by Beijing, the legal and education sector being two of the notable exceptions. The whole election system is designed to ensure that Beijing loyalists, despite having never commanded the popular vote, always have a majority in the chamber.

In 2016 I decided to run for election to Hong Kong's Legislative Council. It would be the first Legco election since the 2014 protests and the Umbrella Movement, and the failure of the Hong Kong government to pass Beijing's controversial electoral reform package. It was an important test of the direction a new democratic movement would take. Would my generation, angered by changes to their home and politically inspired by the struggles of 2014, be willing to engage in the political process? Or would the failure of the protests to achieve real democratic reform, coupled with the resulting crackdown and an increasingly hard-line government stance, extinguish hope? Could Hong Kong's engineered political system bring about the changes the city so desperately needed? At the heart of all these questions was the same troubling thought: did people still believe that 'One Country, Two Systems' could work?

The question was taking on increasing urgency. That year, three Hong Kong booksellers who had gone missing the year before reappeared in China. News came to light that they had been kidnapped and brought to the Mainland, where they were interrogated and likely drugged and tortured. The Hong Kong government, still in theory autonomous, was nevertheless powerless to investigate the case or demand answers from Beijing. The case was significant enough for the British government to declare it a breach of the Sino–British Joint Declaration. Beijing, casually oblivious to the feelings and insecurities of Hong Kong people, simply reiterated its line that the treaty was a 'historic document'.

I knew as a student activist that my perspective was reflective of the overwhelming majority of my generation. So-called 'pragmatists' and loyal Beijing elites deride us as spoilt, materialistic and apolitical – a charge that reflects not on the young but on themselves, and ironically on the type of citizen Beijing seems keen to promote. I could see for myself that this was absurdly untrue. My generation were raised to view Hong Kong not only as our home but also as our only point of reference. We related to and cared for Hong Kong in a way that was not represented by our pro-Beijing political elite.

I believe the young should have ideals. To be able to imagine a better home, and one that is more reflective of our own values and those of today and not the past, is an important freedom of youth. As students we don't yet have many of the responsibilities of later life, and we are also less deeply embedded in existing political power structures. Our relative innocence to the way things are, and to the realities of the world, fosters a refreshing idealism and the imagination to do things differently. We see this in young people everywhere.

How the idealism and hopefulness of youth are treated is reflective of how open, free and responsive a society is. When you live in a society shaped not by its citizens but by the politics of a capital thousands of miles away, and by people who do not even share your language, values or political culture, hope is especially important. It allows us to look afresh at the challenges we face, uncompromised by the status quo. The young see problems for what they are and question the presumptions on which injustices thrive and should be a spearhead for change. After all, it is they who will inherit the world we are making today.

As a young public figure, I was aware that many people of my age could relate to my story. I did not come from the elite, nor did my family move in those circles. As a student activist I had already spent years engaging with people from every background and political persuasion, developing the skills a politician should have. I was always open. Sometimes these interactions could be disappointingly unsophisticated; others were heated. But these experiences helped me develop empathy, and inform my understanding of the issues as they were felt by the people. Most of all, they confirmed to me that I was not alone in how I felt about my home city, what I valued and how I saw things going in Hong Kong. Many, many people felt the same way as I did – and none felt they had a voice.

Together with my friends and fellow activists Joshua Wong, Agnes Chow and Ivan Lam, I co-founded a new political party called Demosisto. We would be a fresh, youth-led party appealing to and representing a new generation – younger, more dynamic and less elite than more established pro-democracy parties.

As a political organization, we were very careful about how we positioned ourselves. Compared with other new political parties being formed to contest the election, we were moderate. We had worked with, and continued to work within, the more conservative pan-democratic camp, from whom we knew we had much to learn. Decades of engagement with the authorities, including with Beijing, had failed to achieve anything substantive for democracy in Hong Kong and had compromised and split these traditional parties. Dominated by lawyers and professionals, the moderate politics they represented seemed increasingly a relic of another, more hopeful time. They were, to a younger generation, 'old-fashioned' politicians shaped by the more polite politics of the colonial era. To push paper with the government may have worked at one time, but the CCP is not the British administration. These parties, who were shedding support, understood this too. They understood as we did the need to reinvent the democratic movement, and were keen to engage with us in doing so. While we respected what they had done and what we could learn from their experience, we were also eager not to be drawn into the politics of the past that they represented.

Demosisto thus provided a link between these traditional parties and the younger, more radical local politics that was emerging in response to Beijing's politics of nationalism and identity. We never claimed to be a radical or localist party. We didn't even pretend we had the answers, which is why we worked closely with the democratic camp and other pan-democratic figures. What we did have was popular support and a youthful energy that the traditional parties lacked, and which we hoped might help invigorate the political scene. We could be a voice for, and act as a connection to, the younger generation.

In the aftermath of June 2020, many civil organizations in

Hong Kong, including Demosisto, would disband or focus only on low-profile community work. Pro-Beijing media had consistently accused Demosisto of being a group of dangerous 'secessionists', agents of 'hostile foreign forces' and the 'black hand' behind the Hong Kong pro-democracy protest movement. Contrary to these later smears, we never advocated for a Hong Kong with an independent sovereignty. We only pointed to the rights Hong Kong was due under its own constitution. We believed in honouring this agreement in letter and in spirit. Hong Kong people deserved those rights, which had already been guaranteed and promised to us by Beijing. We also believed that Hong Kong people should determine the city's future and governing system. The CCP likes to talk about throwing off the shackles of imperialism, and that was exactly what we were doing. In August 2016, a month before the election, our team were starting to worry. The polls suggested I had little support in the constituency I was running in. Hong Kong Island is a wealthy and generally conservative district, known for electing prominent members of Hong Kong's professional and elite class – lawyers, public intellectuals and former government officials. To make things more difficult, my constituency happened to have the highest number of elderly residents. It was also an important 'super seat' that would return six places in the legislature by proportional representation, so fifteen parties had fielded candidates.

While we were hopeful, our expectations were low. I may have been a public figure, but I was known only as a student activist. Going straight from student activism to the first tier of Hong Kong politics was not easy. I had to adjust my mindset. I was no longer representing students like me, but having to appeal to and present myself as someone who could represent a much broader range of people. I needed to demonstrate that I had the ability to understand the complexity of realpolitik, and accommodate the diverse needs and views of constituents. I also had to convince people that I was able to represent them in the city's highest chamber. In the last two weeks of the election, I worked as hard as I could to outline my beliefs and analyse heated debates about policy. I wanted to prove that age, education and experience are not the deciding factors in what constitutes a proper lawmaker: determination, vision and eloquence are what matter most.

The 2016 election saw an unprecedented turnout: 2.2 million voters, 58 per cent of the registered electorate, cast their vote. Despite the constant hectoring of Beijing's loyalists, the silent majority had spoken, and it was in favour of pro-democracy candidates. A new force had emerged in local politics, with new, progressive localist candidates winning six seats. And I won my seat, by a far greater margin than polls had suggested, to become Hong Kong's youngest-ever lawmaker.

I was so proud of what we had achieved. We had exercised our right to stand for election, and in voting for us the people of Hong Kong had exercised their right to elect representatives who shared their concerns. The legislature may have been designed to ensure a pro-establishment majority, making it more of a debating chamber than a true law-making body. But to be one of thirty-five directly elected legislators still mattered. My election represented an expression of the limited political rights Hong Kong people enjoyed – an expression of our freedom. I had a democratic mandate and no one in government could claim otherwise. Even if all I could do was be one voice in the chamber, this voice would be heard throughout the city; and for so many people of my generation, and for all those who had voted for me, that mattered.

At twenty-three years of age, I was Hong Kong's youngest legislator. Often, babies of the House, as the youngest parliamentarians are called in the UK, go on to have long careers in politics. Mine in Hong Kong would be one of the shortest.

Legislative Council members are elected to serve a four-year term. As my team moved into our new offices in the Legislative Council Complex, there was no reason to suppose we would not be there for at least that long. We did our best to make ourselves feel comfortable in room 901. As an activist I had met and worked with many legislators, but to be sitting in the Council building now as one of them felt different. I watched political aides come and go, and my staff hovering busily about, and could not help but wonder if I truly belonged there. Was this the right place for an activist? Could it accommodate us?

Well-known democratic lawmakers stopped by to welcome me. They did their best to make me feel I belonged. Many were politicians and campaigners I looked up to and had worked with during the protests. They had fought hard for a better Hong Kong – for labour rights, civil liberties and for other important freedoms. Still, any pride I might have felt was overridden by the realization of what I was up against. Though my allies in the democratic camp were capable and respected in the wider community, they were operating within a system designed to ensure they would never have power. And those who did have power would seek to silence and destroy us.

My election had been a terrible loss of face for Beijing and their loyal supporters. It shattered one of their principal lies: that the majority of Hong Kong people are loyal patriots who place the 'nation' (meaning the CCP) over local issues and a desire for freedom and democracy. It was a lie that had served the interests of the powerful, from the officials and secret Communist Party members who dominated Hong Kong's elites to international businesses who had throughout Hong Kong's history suppressed the will of the people in order to promote so-called stability and a favourable commercial environment. It was a lie that Hong Kong's last governor, Chris Patten, had bravely challenged by going directly to the people, refusing the assurances of an elite who insisted that Hong Kong people were apolitical. It was a lie that had become increasingly pernicious as Beijing encroached on our freedoms, making democratic representation even more important. And my presence in the Legislative Council, alongside other new and progressive lawmakers, told the world that it was a lie. Beijing would not forgive me for that.

The Oath

When the law ceases to be independent, when the authority of the courts is subordinate to politics, when judges must be patriots and the law acts in the service of political authority, we have rule by law. When this happens, the law is no longer pursuing justice; instead it becomes a tool for persecution and oppression. The tendrils of authoritarianism creep up on us slowly, strangling the institutions that safeguard us and challenging our values until we are too exhausted to resist.

Before assuming office, all legislators must swear allegiance to the PRC and to uphold Hong Kong's constitution. While this is a solemn act, there was also a long-standing tradition that allowed legislators to make political statements during the oath-taking ceremony. This usually happened either immediately before or after swearing the oath of office. It was an important opportunity for new legislators to state their personal political beliefs, and it was not uncommon for pro-democracy legislators to take this opportunity to declare their determination to fight for their cause. This was, after all, what they had been elected to do.

Although never codified, I shared the view that was commonly understood: that this was a legitimate expression of our freedom of speech. There was nothing in the Basic Law that expressly prohibited it. I therefore discussed with my team how best I might make use of this opportunity. We decided that I should quote from people who inspire me, and who could best encapsulate my beliefs and the type of politician I am. Knowing it might be a sensitive matter, we sought legal advice at every stage to ensure we would not be crossing any lines.

On 12 October 2016, I took my turn to take my oath of office at the Legislative Council. In the chamber a large oak desk stood on the platform beneath the President's chair. Two Council Secretaries stood on either side, holding the documents from which we were to read. It was their job to approve that the oath had been taken.

I was the last legislator to swear the oath. I witnessed all sixty-nine other legislators approach the podium and perform the ritual. Many had, not unexpectedly, taken the opportunity to issue their own statements.

When my turn came, I was calm. I was very conscious of the simple leather umbrella-shaped necklace around my neck – the symbol of the democratic movement. I wanted to remind everyone watching that I remained an activist and would not back down from expressing what I believed was right and true now that I was inside the system.

As I stood to take my oath, I declared that I would not simply obey a regime that brutally kills its people. I served not the political aggression of a regime, but the people. I then quoted Mahatma Gandhi:

> You can chain me, you can torture me, you can even destroy this body, but you will never imprison my mind.

As I took the oath of office, I was careful to read each word with clarity. I didn't deviate from the script:

> I will uphold the Basic Law of the Hong Kong Special Administrative Region of the People's Republic of China, bear allegiance to the Hong Kong Special Administrative Region of the People's Republic of China.

Yet in my heart I could not help but feel the contradiction between carrying a popular mandate and swearing allegiance to a regime that silences its people. I could not help but raise the tone of my voice as I said, 'People's Republic of China'.

In my mind I kept returning to that quote by Gandhi, which now revealed a new meaning: I may be a legislator, and part of a political system designed to give Hong Kong the vestige of accountability as Beijing hollowed out its identity by stealth, but I would not be co-opted by the trappings of office. I would continue, and must continue, to represent my people and to speak truth to power.

My oath was accepted by the ratifier and approved by the Secretary General of the Secretariat of the Legislative Council of Hong Kong. The President of the Legislative Council did not challenge the legitimacy of my oath. I was confirmed as a member of the Legislative Council and could officially carry out my responsibilities as a legislator.

But Beijing intervened. It claimed an unelected and unaccountable political authority to 'reinterpret' Article 104 of the Basic Law, altering the requirements for taking the oath. In the new interpretation, lawmakers must not only swear allegiance to Hong Kong as part of China, but the law even describes how they should do it, and the consequences of failing to do so. It requires the oath-taker to be 'solemn' – which can be arbitrarily defined by the government.

Shockingly, Beijing decided to apply this reinterpretation retroactively. This violates a fundamental principle of the rule of law: clearly, people cannot violate laws that are not yet made. I had taken my oath in accordance with the law as it was at the time of taking, and with respect to the way the ceremony was understood.

Having casually redefined the constitution, Beijing now demanded (in the name of the rule of law!) that the Hong Kong authorities apply this new understanding to have me and other pro-democracy legislators disqualified. Nine months after being officially confirmed as a legislator and carrying out my duties, I was stripped of my rights and removed from the chamber.

Beijing's new interpretation was effectively an amendment to the existing law. Yet by insisting on it being an 'interpretation', the law could be applied retroactively. Beijing declared that everyone in Hong Kong had previously misread and misunderstood the law, after almost twenty years of common agreement. That the law had already been interpreted and applied differently seemed not to matter, nor was Beijing concerned about so publicly undermining Hong Kong's judiciary and the competence of the city's legal profession. As it was a 'clarification', the courts had no option but to rule in accordance with the CCP's political decision.

To the dismay of many Hongkongers, six democratic legislators were disqualified. This was the exact number the pro-Beijing camp needed to ensure the democrats could not hold up legislation in the chamber. I was one of them.

How can anyone live their life if they are asked to obey laws that don't yet exist? And what does the law even represent if its interpretation becomes arbitrary and fluid, dependent on the whims of those in power? In such a society there is only one law left: the right of the powerful to oppress the weak.

Hong Kong's Fundamental Contradiction

The Oath-Taking Controversy, as it became known, high-lighted the fundamental contradiction in Hong Kong's legal system. You cannot have rule of law when the law is itself at the mercy of a system that neither respects nor practises the rule of law. While the Sino–British Joint Declaration bound China to accepting the continuation of British common law in Hong Kong until at least 2047, by giving Beijing the final say in interpretation of the law, Hong Kong's courts are ultimately not arbiters of the law but executors.

Beijing is eager to point out that, by law, it has the ultimate right of interpretation; but under the Basic Law, for an interpretation to be made all three of the following criteria must be met:

1. The interpretation must concern the responsibilities of Beijing or the relationship between Beijing and Hong Kong.
2. It must be issued at the request of the Hong Kong Court of Final Appeal (CFA), except when concerning China's sovereignty.
3. It must be an interpretation of the law, and not an amendment.

Needless to say, these three criteria are not being met. One of the more important interpretations in relation to Hong Kong's freedoms and democratic aspirations was back in 2004, when Beijing issued two critical amendments giving them more power to influence the appointment of the Chief Executive, who runs the city. This intervention was not invited by Hong Kong's Court of Final Appeal, nor was it merely an interpretation. The decision was monumental. The PRC had assumed sovereignty of Hong Kong with a promise of autonomy and of democratic change. This was a promise made not only to Britain but, more importantly, to the Hong Kong people, who had accepted the change without being consulted in the process. The promise kept the democratic aspirations of the people alive, and framed a role for democratic politicians within the system to work with Beijing in formulating a road map to an agreed goal. All faith in that process was dashed – not at the point of a gun but with the stroke of a pen.

While the courts were granted some liberty to continue following common-law principles, constitutional issues were now the domain of the national government. For Beijing, the law provides not a consideration of the limits of their authority, but a means by which they might interfere with, control and dominate Hong Kong.

With each new interpretation, the space in which the rule of law in Hong Kong exists shrinks. In the minds of many, the rule of law does not exist as an independent source of authority but by the grace of the CCP. Clearly, it is not how the courts should operate. This has slowly, but fundamentally, eroded our understanding of the rule of law, and our relationship with it.

Without clear guidelines provided by the law we do not know where we stand, or have a clear idea of what role we can play. If the constitution is open to 'reinterpretation' at any time, we lose that critical level of certainty required to feel at ease. The regime can easily weaponize the law and prosecute individuals who challenge its hegemony.

After Beijing asserted its right to reinterpret the law, the more principled judges, such as Justice Kemal Bokhary had been during the controversy, would later be notably absent from the Court of Appeal. The undesirable need to balance questions of legal principle with the interests of the CCP – to accept that the only way to protect the greater body of the rule of law is to accept compromises in principle – politicizes the law to the detriment of citizens. So although Hong Kong's judges are able, well trained and materially incorruptible, they are mere executors of a system that is fundamentally flawed. Though the judiciary might try its best, it is not and cannot be a guardian of Hong Kong's rights and freedoms.

History teaches us that an impartial court cannot exist if it isn't empowered to depart from the position of the political authorities. The rule of law does not exist in a society that is led to believe that the law serves patriotism, and where pragmatism is valued more highly than principle.

Reclaiming Civic Square

Since 2014, I have regularly been arrested. The police will often target me and other prominent activists at protests. I am arrested and then detained in a police station to await bail. Most of the time, bail will be granted and I will be released, as the police have no grounds to prosecute me.

At other times the police press charges anyway, despite not having sufficient evidence to get a conviction. Even though the charges brought against me and other activists may be dismissed in court, the process of being prosecuted and having to go to court is arduous and demoralizing, especially for young people who have no criminal record. In this way, the actions of the state prosecutors have a chilling effect on anyone who dares to speak up when they witness injustice.

In 2015 I was charged, along with Joshua Wong, for obstructing a police officer. The case related to an incident thirteen months earlier, at a peaceful protest Joshua and I were at outside China's Liaison Office in Hong Kong. Obstruction is not easy to define, and on the day we received no warning that our actions might be construed as such. We were simply exercising our right to peaceful protest. However, Hong Kong was already changing fast, and Joshua and I were marked men.

It was the first time I had been brought to court, and I found it a tiring and stressful experience. After my arrest I was released on bail. My photograph and fingerprints were taken, and I underwent interrogation; I had to seek legal assistance and apply for legal aid as, being a university student, I could not afford a lawyer; and I had to report back to the police station regularly. It took me a long time to collect all the documents I needed to apply for legal aid, and then to prepare for my case. Under the political circumstances, there was also the fear that my application for legal aid would be rejected or that the assistance provided to me would be withdrawn.

Given the lack of evidence the police could present, the court dismissed the case. In hindsight this should not have come as a surprise, but at the time you are still racked by the thought that the court might rule against you. I didn't want to take any chances and spent all my time preparing for the case. During the trial I felt stressed and exhausted, both physically and mentally. The time Joshua and I spent tied up with needless paperwork was not lost on the authorities.

The following year I was again in court. This time I was charged with 'inciting unlawful assembly' for my role in the occupation of Civic Square in September 2014. The case was particularly symbolic because the action initiated the Umbrella Movement.

Along with activists and student leaders, I was part of a crowd that had scaled the railings erected around the square before gathering in the centre in peaceful protest. The protestors with me were mostly young men and women, many of them students, and each of us carried little more than a rucksack with snacks and bottled water. No one was armed. No one acted aggressively. The aim was simply to occupy the square and sit peacefully in protest. Our demand was for Beijing to fulfil the promises it had made to the Hong Kong people: basically, a demand to honour a treaty obligation and respect the rule of law.

It was hoped that international media would pick up on the protest, and therefore raise the profile of Hong Kong's situation globally and within the business community, which had been notably absent in the debate on democracy in Hong Kong (and often actively complicit in Beijing's growing influence in the city). However – and this was stressed from the beginning – the movement was local, locally supported and locally driven, to avoid giving credence to the standard line

Beijing rolls out that any criticism is the result of 'black hands' and 'foreign interference'. Initially, we did not actively engage with foreign media. This only changed when it became clear that neither the Hong Kong government nor Beijing were prepared to enter into a dialogue. Looking back, this strategy was basically futile because Beijing does not care about the reality – it discredits all opposition in this way, without reference to what its critics have done in the real world. Today, international advocacy is a critically important part of Hong Kong's democratic movement, but only because all domestic avenues for engagement have been closed off.

Occupy Central with Love and Peace was never supposed to happen. It was the final stage of a process of engagement with the authorities which the organizers Tai, Chu and their colleague Chan Kin-man hoped would be successful – the stick that would draw Beijing to the table in a meaningful way and help drive a solution. Ten stages of engagement were laid out over the course of eighteen months. The protest would only be necessary should all other stages fail.

In June 2014, three months before the protest, China's State Council issued a white paper redefining the promised high degree of autonomy as merely 'the power to run local affairs as authorized by the central leadership'. This in turn redefined the city's authorities. They were no longer Hong Kong's representatives working with Beijing, they were simply Beijing's bureaucrats in Hong Kong. Political authority came from the CCP. There was no place for the Sino–British Joint Declaration, which provided a framework for the autonomy and rights that Hongkongers were to enjoy under the 'One Country, Two Systems' formula until 2047. Beijing had already begun recasting the treaty as a 'historic document' – a position rejected by Britain and inconsistent with the fact that the treaty remains registered with the United Nations.

Then, on 31 August, Beijing's Standing Committee redefined the meaning of universal suffrage by stipulating 'institutional safeguards' that ensured only candidates approved by Beijing could stand. Hong Kong's Chief Executive was to be chosen by committee and appointed by Beijing. So, while people were technically being granted the right to vote for the Chief Executive, it would not be a free choice. Worse, Beijing could claim that the 'winning' candidate had a popular mandate. Even with the promise that all Legco seats would be directly elected, no one believed the CCP would honour its words now. For many Hong Kong people, Beijing had broken its word too often to be believed, and the proposed reform, and the way Beijing sought to frame it, only confirmed their fears.

Civic Square was designed and designated as a public space, as the name implies. Reclaiming the square was therefore not only significant within the context of the pro-democracy student protests that had already begun around the Legislative Council Complex, it was also about reclaiming our civil rights as Hong Kong citizens and reconnecting with a space that had been important to protestors.

If, in reclaiming the square, we were acting within the spirit of what Hong Kong had been – and could be – the police response and that of the authorities signalled how Hong Kong had changed. Images of young protestors being manhandled by the police out of the square angered many people. It was not that it was brutal but that it was disproportionate, and out of keeping with what people had come to expect. The authorities deployed riot police. This was not to tackle violence, but to break up the protest – although there had been no violence, nor any reason to presume the protests would turn that way.

A friend described receiving a call from his elderly relatives, who had previously encouraged family members to avoid politics, now telling him to join the protest. His relatives were in tears when they said: 'What the police are doing is wrong. It is not the Hong Kong way. You must go. Represent the family.'

Despite this, the day following my arrest saw hundreds of thousands of people gathered in protest outside the Legislative Council Complex calling for 'genuine universal suffrage'. This mattered not only as an ideal, or out of respect for what was enshrined in law, but because the authoritarian application of power meant there was now an acute need for genuine representation. Unable to trust the authorities to govern in their best interest, now more than ever Hongkongers needed an accountable government.

What happened was not a planned act of civil disobedience but a spontaneous protest against a changing Hong Kong. There were students rejecting Beijing's attempt to redefine core concepts on which our freedoms and way of life were founded; young people and young families who rejected Beijing's alternative reality, fearing they had no future in a city increasingly focused on serving China over the needs of its own people; the educated classes, the traditional support base for Hong Kong's democratic movement, exhausted of good faith and despondent after seventeen years of attempting to work with Beijing in fulfilling its obligations. Whether driven by ideals or bitter experience, in hope for the future or in reaction to the past, or for reasons of local identity or universal values, people were united by a shared understanding that Hong Kong was changing fundamentally, and not for the better. Now, more than ever, freedom and democracy mattered.

The response of the authorities to a tentative crowd was batons and tear gas, tactics not used against Hong Kong residents since the 1967 Cultural Revolution-inspired (and CCP-supported) Hong Kong riots. Back then, protestors carried firearms, people were killed and Hong Kong was facing a bombing campaign that left scores of innocent people dead.

In 2014, by contrast, the police faced unarmed civilians sitting in the street, singing songs. Riot police were deployed against a generation in Hong Kong who knew no violence. What made the Hong Kong Police Force prep their officers to face a war zone and to see protestors as hostile?

Some began to fear that the culture within the police was changing – that loyalty was being placed above competence. The increasingly political nature of senior appointments and growing links with Mainland security forces now started to look sinister. It was the actions of the police, not the protestors, that played to these fears.

The disproportionate use of force on that first day did not put people off from attending protests in the streets. Instead, it sustained the hurt and anger that would mobilize the population for seventy-nine consecutive days. The umbrella, which was used to shield protestors from tear gas and baton charges, became a protest symbol.

It is said that while it takes many years of good service to build a reputation, one act of madness can destroy it. If the Hong Kong Police Force had admitted these early mistakes, accepted that they had misread the situation and agreed to an independent inquiry, public confidence in them may have remained high. Likewise, if the Hong Kong government had sought to engage with the protestors with empathy and respect, openly acknowledge the past failings of the political process and confirm that it comprised not only bureaucrats but also representatives of the people, the protests would not have continued as they did. Both institutions instead chose to make an enemy of the protestors, to try to turn the community on itself. In doing so they only confirmed the protestors' worst fears: Hong Kong really had taken an authoritarian turn.

For my role at the start of the 2014 protests I was sentenced to 120 hours of community service in the first trial. I accepted this. I had broken the law. Nevertheless, it was hard to process the idea that I was now a criminal. To have broken the law felt so alien to me. While I was prepared to face my sentence, as all activists who confront unjust laws must be, I was nevertheless irritated by the irony of such acts of civil disobedience – that in order to advocate for democracy and justice and safeguard the rule of law, sometimes laws had to be broken.

Motivation and context are important in maintaining the spirit of the law. This was reflected in the judge's declaration:

When the youth violate the law to express opinions, besides taking the actions and the incurred consequences into consideration, we should adopt a more lenient and understanding attitude, to discern the motives behind their violations.

The ruling was, however, challenged by the pro-Beijing camp and Chinese state media, who demanded that all protestors and activists receive severe punishment. This challenge to Hong Kong's independent judiciary, this demand that judges be loyal to the Party and act on political considerations, was made in the name of the rule of law.

It was disappointing that the Department of Justice had felt the need to seek my prosecution in any way it could. I am not a hardened criminal, nor does my freedom pose a public threat. Even more disappointing was its decision to file an appeal against the way our case had been sentenced. Joshua Wong, Alex Chow and I were asked to accept the verdict in the Court of Appeal in August 2017, one month after I was to be evicted from the Legislative Council. The authorities were utilizing a legal trio well known to authoritarian regimes:

1. Arrest, detention and interrogation by the police.
2. Charges are pressed by the prosecutors despite a lack of evidence, and with little regard for the law or public safety.
3. The court and if possible the judiciary itself is pressured into making a political ruling, even at the expense of legal precedent.

In 2019, the Hong Kong Police brought criminal charges against all nine organizers of the 2014 pro-democracy protests, including the seventy-five-year-old Reverend Chu. All had turned themselves in to the police voluntarily and were prepared to be held responsible under the law for their actions. That after five years a rarely used colonial-era public nuisance charge was all that could be mustered suggests this was not about protecting society, but about punishment. What purpose could our imprisonment serve? Finding a way to prosecute someone under law does not make a prosecution just. This is what we mean when we say that the rule of law is about understanding why those laws were made, and whom they serve.

Even a good system, applied and exercised professionally by a legal culture steeped in understanding, can be corrupted. The rule of law takes a generation to build, and even if the process remains on paper it too can be dismantled within a generation as people unlearn its meaning. Without the protection of democracy, the rule of law is a fortress built on a foundation of shifting sand. No matter how impregnable it may appear, it slips further each day.

A legal system is meant to protect the individual from oppression by the powerful. It is meant to place rights above interests. There are many who will claim that as long as you don't get involved in politics, everything is fine and nothing will change. Many of those who do business or invest in Hong Kong like to say this. But to be apolitical is the luxury of a free society. Under the CCP, the line between what is political and what is not can shift overnight, as many of China's most successful business leaders are finding out.

Beijing likes to talk about 'rule according to law'. The CCP, like all authoritarian regimes, sees the legal system as an extension of the regime, a tool that should be designed and applied in the service of its political interests. China no longer recognizes the importance of preserving the rule of law or an independent court – a strategy by which the CCP retained the trust of Hong Kong people and international businesses decades ago. But it no longer needs the smokescreen of judicial independence – the CCP is confident in its economic might and political power.

Whom Does the Law Serve?

Like most people, while I was growing up I was taught to always abide by the law. I was told that the law establishes the parameters between right and wrong. The justice system is there to punish those who cross the line into doing wrong. The law is about maintaining stability in society, so we can all live peaceably.

Such an understanding of the law is fine for a child. It keeps us on the straight and narrow. But there comes a point when simply telling people what they must and must not do is not enough, and reasoning becomes important. We begin to understand that laws are not equivalent to justice – they are how justice is achieved, a means, not an end. What if the government decides to use the legal system to serve a purpose other than justice?

This sort of question should come naturally to us as we develop critical faculties. We begin to see the law not simply as a set of rules written in stone, but as a man-made system that can take on many forms and functions. As we explore this we learn to distinguish between just and unjust laws, and between the rule of law and rule by law. We understand, too, that the law is not perfect and that justice is an ideal, and that every generation must fight to hold on to it, like all ideals. We see the failings of even the better systems of law to provide justice, whether because of high fees and long trials or institutional failings that affect the way cases are tried. But we can also, I hope, distinguish between an imperfect system and one that is inherently, and often by design, unjust.

Sadly, unjust legal systems persist in many countries around the world. For instance, Thailand's *lèse-majesté* law, officially known as Section 112 of the Criminal Code, is used to prosecute critics of the Thai royal family, including pro-democracy activists, as part of a deliberate strategy. The law prohibits criticism, insult or defamation of the Thai monarchy. While similar laws are still preserved in many other countries, most states treat them as symbolic and rarely, if ever, exercise them. When they are considered, it is usually within the context of current mores and applied in a way consistent with other rights protected in law.

In 2014, the elected government of Thailand was overthrown in a military coup and the junta passed a draft constitution in 2016. Military representatives enjoy complete dominance in the Thai Senate and control all the most important roles in government.

The current King of Thailand, Maha Vajiralongkorn, is very unpopular. His behaviour might charitably be described as eccentric. He lives mostly in Germany, where he has been photographed cycling with his entourage in tank tops and less. He used to dress up his pet dog, Foo Foo, as an air chief marshal and take him to formal events. Married four times, he is believed to have fathered seven children with three different women, and had the parents of his third wife, a lady-in-waiting named Srirasmi, jailed for allegedly abusing their connections with him. In actions and in attitude he seems indifferent to his own people. However, Thailand remains a constitutional monarchy, and the royal family continue to hold significant power to influence governance. In truth, the king may have had no choice when he bestowed his blessing on the military junta, but in so doing he legitimated military rule and reforms that have rolled back many civil rights Thai citizens once enjoyed, shifting Thailand firmly towards authoritarianism.

First a court order was produced to dissolve the pro-democracy Future Power Party, provoking widespread protests. People demanded the dissolution of the military-dominated legislature, that a new constitution be drafted and for more scrutiny of the royal family. In response, the royal family and military junta reacted brutally. Among the tools they used were the *lèse-majesté* law.

In court proceedings, no benefit of doubt was recognized and bail was routinely rejected. Under the law, people were arbitrarily arrested and detained in violation of international human rights law. Penalties per offence ranged from three to fifteen years' imprisonment. One arrestee, accused of twenty-nine counts of violating the law, faced a possible eighty-seven years in prison. By pleading guilty, her sentence was reduced to forty-three years.* Her crime was to have posted videos online deemed insulting of the royal family.

Since the 2014 coup, ninety-eight people have been

---

* 'Thai court sentences woman to 43 years for insulting monarchy', https://www.ft.com/content/9185bf2c-6f5a-4c5a-ac68-cef303450852

charged under Thailand's *lèse-majesté* law. To quote Patsara-valee Tanakitvibulpon, a twenty-five-year-old engineering student and pro-democracy activist:

> *I am not afraid. I understand that invoking this law is the government's plan to suppress us.*

> *I think it is illegitimate to enforce this law . . . to obstruct people's freedom to speak the truth even though there are now many accusations about royal involvement in politics.*

Despite such oppression, people continue to protest. As happened in Hong Kong, and elsewhere in the world where there is rising authoritarianism, from Myanmar to Syria and from Belarus to Turkey, rising oppression deepens resentment. Some will lie low, but the sense of injustice burns in their hearts. As Thomas Jefferson noted, when injustice becomes law, resistance becomes a duty.

In August 2020 I was reminded again of the way in which the law can be corrupted, and by the deep well of human spirit we can all draw on to resist. I was in Berlin to protest the meeting of Chinese Foreign Minister Wang Yi with his German counterpart, Heiko Maas. I wanted to ensure that recent events in Hong Kong would be noted. Several journalists asked me whether I was afraid for my life. Alexei Navalny, the Russian opposition leader, lawyer and anti-corruption campaigner, was at the time fighting for his life in a hospital only a few blocks from my hotel. He had been poisoned with a banned chemical that suggested that he was a victim of the Russian state.

I told the reporters I could not rule out the possibility that I too might be targeted, but that I was no longer afraid, merely aware. When you are wanted by an autocratic state with no respect for the law (nor constrained by common decency), such things may happen. As a 'national enemy' as defined by the Chinese government, I accept that my life will be lived in the shadow of constant threats and intimidation. Even in exile the danger continues – both Russia and China have a record of not respecting sovereignty, and of arranging the kidnapping of people from other states.

Soon after Navalny had recovered, he chose to return to Russia. Upon landing he told waiting media, who were surprised that he would further endanger himself by returning to his homeland, 'I know that I'm right. I fear nothing.' Shortly after that, he was arrested and accused of violating parole conditions.

No matter how absurd it may seem to imprison someone for failing to fulfil their parole requirement when they were in a coma and receiving life-saving treatment in another country, the Putin regime was determined to do it. In February 2021, a Moscow court overruled his suspended sentence and sentenced him to a further two and a half years in jail.

The words of Navalny, as he stood in court, resonate far beyond the borders of Russia:

> The main thing in this whole trial isn't what happens to me. Locking me up isn't difficult . . . What matters most is why this is happening. This is happening to intimidate large numbers of people. This is how it works: imprison one person

to frighten millions . . . This is what happens when
lawlessness and tyranny become the essence of a political
system, and it's horrifying. But it's even worse when
lawlessness and tyranny pose as state prosecutors and dress
up in judges' robes . . . It's the duty of every person to defy
*you and to defy such laws.**

The practice of using seemingly mundane laws to camou-flage what is in fact political persecution has a long history in many authoritarian countries. As in Navalny's case, corrup-tion is an easy charge to level in a system that is inherently corrupt. In China, too, corruption is an excuse to purge polit-ical rivals. Tax 'irregularities' hit business people. Often some sort of sexual deviancy is added to truly destroy the victim's reputation, and to play to a more primal revulsion in the pub-lic. The uniquely Chinese offence of 'provoking quarrels' is a favourite for arresting artists, petitioners or lawyers who fail to toe the line. Coerced video confessions are broadcast on state-owned television channels, where the accused are made to read aloud scripts prepared by the state security apparatus to 'prove' to the public that they are 'genuine wrongdoers'. This may seem anathema to those of us who have been brought up in a free society with the rule of law. It was cer-tainly so for Hong Kong people.

---

* 'Vladimir the Poisoner of Underpants', https://www.nytimes.com/2021/02/03/opinion/navalny-putin-speech.html

Looking Behind the Law

In political debates, the term 'law and order' is often thought of in connection with law enforcement and the legal system. It presumes laws to be just, and a well-functioning legal system to be one where courts rule purely on the law and police enforce the law without question. But the reality is that laws are not always just, and justice itself evolves as our values change. Laws must be understood, applied and enforced in context.

To review and pass laws we need competent and accountable legislators. Laws need updating to be relevant. Lately, and across the world, new technologies are challenging us to rethink how our laws work and whether new laws are necessary to protect our rights. Laws are not perfect, and we should not shy away from questioning – and if necessary challenging – them if we are to apply the law correctly.

Convicted of illegal assembly, I was first sentenced to community service. After an appeal by the Department of Justice, my sentence was changed to imprisonment and I was sentenced to eight months in jail. I then had to appeal against their appeal and was eventually released, but only after I had already served two months. As with my friend Joshua Wong, the Department of Justice was looking beyond prosecution – it had become persecution.

Hong Kong had crossed a line and was fast on its way towards rule by law. Whenever a judgment of the courts is overturned through a political reinterpretation of the constitution, justice lies not with the Hong Kong courts but with the Politburo in Beijing. The law ceases to exist in parallel with political power and loses its ability to act as a check.

Beijing effectively controls the appointment of high-ranking judges by overseeing the system of internal promotion. It can place demands on judges to be patriots and to pledge allegiance not to the rule of law or the constitution but to the CCP and to the People's Republic. It sees no issue with threatening lawyers and judges, and openly criticizing their judgements on state media. Taken together, these actions add up.

In China, under the leadership of President Xi Jinping the law has reoriented away from the court system and back towards the Party, the ultimate adjudicator and the source of all jurisdiction. The legal system has reverted from being an independent court system to a Party-centred one in which political ideology takes precedence. In a speech in August 2018, Xi told Party members that China must never follow the path of Western 'constitutionalism', 'separation of powers' or 'judicial independence'. Xi subsequently explained the Chinese way of law, or *fazhi*:

> *We must take up legal weapons, occupy the high point of the rule of law, and say no to the saboteurs and spoilers . . . We need to build up a 'socialist legal team' whose members are loyal to the Party, to the state, to the people, and to the law.*

There is an important lesson in the words of Margaret Ng, one of Hong Kong's finest legal minds and the former Legco member representing the legal sector. The seventy-three-year-old lawyer gave these words in mitigation upon her sentencing for participating in an illegal assembly:

We are mindful that when the court applies a law which
takes away fundamental rights, the confidence in the courts
and judicial independence is shaken, even when the fault lies
in the law, not with the judge who applies it, and that would
strike at the foundation of our rule of law.

It still sounds strange to me to say that I am a convicted criminal. When I was a child, I thought that being a criminal automatically meant you were a bad person. But, like any system created by people, the law is fallible and can only ever serve the interests of its creators. The purpose of the law should be to place limits on power so that people across society can be treated fairly; when this does not happen, we need to ask why.

CHAPTER 5

DISINFORMATION
AND DIVISION

Authoritarianism is on the rise, and authoritarian regimes today are more ambitious and able to exert greater control on public opinion than ever before. Although it was once hoped that technology would set us free, in reality we have allowed the opposite to happen. More choice has not allowed us to get closer to the truth, but confused the picture and diminished the influence of our most accountable and reputable sources of news and information.

In China, information is becoming increasingly controlled and a parallel reality is being created – a reality dictated not by the interests of the people, but by those of the CCP. In this environment, facts are not something to be discovered: they are created to support the official narrative. Thus China's recent claim to islands and atolls in the South China Sea, by which the country claims almost all of this strategically important water-way, are presented as 'indisputable' and 'historic' when they are neither.* Similarly, peaceful protests in Hong Kong are presented as riots, and reasonable local grievance framed as a plot by foreign powers.

In Xinjiang, over a million Uyghurs, an ethnic group persecuted simply for the existence of their culture, are held against their will in what Beijing calls 're-education' camps. At first Beijing denied incarcerating people at all. Then, when it became undeniable, they switched to presenting China's actions as moral and a source of pride – the 're-education' camps, China now claims, are attended voluntarily to provide de-radicalization and vocational training. Open societies are derided as racist or victims of capitalist oppression, and free and independent institutions, such as the press, media regulators and the courts, portrayed as no different to those that are state-controlled.

Beijing no longer only seeks to protect its interests at home: it aims to convince people everywhere that authoritarianism is superior to liberal democracy. And yet in many ways it doesn't live up to its own values, let alone those of the West. Whereas state education is free to at least high school in 'capitalist' countries like the US, UK and in much of Western Europe, in 'socialist' China the government only covers the costs of schooling up to middle school. Many Chinese families have to pay for private tuition and other school expenses, and these outlays are among the highest in the world. As a result, 76 per cent of China's working-age population have not completed high school. Far from focusing on

---

* Bill Hayton, *The South China Sea: The Struggle for Power in Asia* (Yale University Press, 2014)

providing for all of its people, this supposedly 'Communist' country has arguably become the world's most hyper-capitalist and competitive society.

China's Gini coefficient, a measure of inequality that ranges from zero to one, is among the highest in the world. It is officially 0.47, comparable to that of the US. The UK's, the most unequal major state in Europe, has a Gini coefficient of 0.35, Germany 0.29 and Slovenia, the most equal country in the world, scores 0.24. The top 1 per cent in China have a greater share of wealth than the bottom 50 per cent. However, Chinese data is notoriously unreliable, and the real figures are likely much more extreme given the level and scale of corruption. In February 2021, President Xi Jinping declared to much fanfare that China had eliminated absolute poverty – not long before Chinese Premier Li Keqiang cautioned against such hubris, pointing out that the country had more than 600 million people, or 40 per cent of the population, living on $140 per month or less.

Similarly, Chinese diplomats and state media openly portray Western liberal democracies as inherently imperialist, racist and sexist. According to the World Economic Forum's Global Gender Gap Report 2021, which assesses gender disparity across a range of economic, political, educational and health criteria, China ranks 107th out of 144 countries. Chinese women earn approximately 20 per cent less than their male colleagues, and more than 80 per cent of female college graduates report encountering gender discrimination in job searches. Even women's reproductive rights are politicized, with those who say they don't want to get married or have children being viewed as acting against the interests of the Chinese state.

It is common in China for jobs and services to openly specify race and sex. Blackface and other offensive racial stereotyping appears on state-organized national festivals; and a nationwide advert showed a black man falling into a washing machine and being cleaned into an attractive, pale-skinned Chinese man, much to the approval of a leering housewife. In 2020, in an echo of apartheid-era South Africa, the Chinese city of Guangzhou imposed a colour bar across the city. People of colour were refused entry to hospitals, hotels, supermarkets, shops and food outlets, and were subject to compulsory COVID-19 quarantine and testing purely on account of their ethnicity.* Racist comments every bit as vicious as those that appear anywhere in the world are posted daily on Chinese social media, and yet, unlike in the West, and despite the Chinese government's censorship and control, these messages are allowed to remain and are not challenged. There have been no apologies, let alone an inquiry or investigation into racism, sexism or any other form of discrimination. There are no laws in China against racial or sexual discrimination, because as China says, it is a Western problem. According to Beijing, these issues are the lies of 'Western media'.†

In this way and countless others, we are no longer in the realm of disagreement. This is a war on reality, and the only

---

* 'The coronavirus crisis has exposed China's long history of racism', https://www.theguardian.com/commentisfree/2020/apr/25/coronavirus-exposed-china-history-racism-africans-guangzhou
† 'From Covid to Blackface on TV, China's Racism Problem Runs Deep', https://www.hrw.org/news/2021/02/18/covid-blackface-tv-chinas-racism-problem-runs-deep

parties which stand to benefit are rising totalitarian countries like China and Russia. Meanwhile, there are also battle lines being drawn within Western democracies that paint opposition to the regime not just as mistaken but as morally unconscionable. In the case of Hong Kong, and my personal experience, we can easily observe how this can tear a society apart, polarize opinion and stir hatred. We all take different paths through life, but we need to live in a society where there is at least enough accountability to believe what we are told, and enough trust for us to be able to look one another in the eye.

Divergent Paths

In 2017, when passing through the security gate at the entrance to the Legislative Council building, I bumped into an old school friend. I was then still a legislator, and on my way into my offices. She was on her way out. Dressed formally, she was leaving the building on official business.

The security guards on duty at the gate greeted me by name. On hearing my name, she instinctively looked up as we passed, and in that moment I could see in her eyes that spark of recognition. Happy to see an old friend, I smiled and nodded a greeting. However, knowing me seemed to embarrass her. She awkwardly laboured a smile before hurrying out of the building, taking care to avoid my eyes.

Her reaction did not surprise me. It is sadly all too common now. Politics has affected personal relationships in Hong

Kong to the point where people aligned with the powerful see the ones challenging them as the bugs of society.

The moralization of politics feeds polarization. It is a feeling that many will understand, whether in Britain over Brexit or in the increasingly partisan politics of the US and elsewhere. It is healthy to disagree about how we see a problem and how we intend to address it. In a democratic and free society all sides have a voice, and power is not held in a monopoly. Even if the government of the day fails to live up to our expectations, that ideal continues to define the system in spirit.

But what happens when the political divide crosses a moral red line? And when the choice we face is not between divergent solutions to a common problem, but between states of existence – between being a free and open society and one which is closed, dictated and oppressive?

The encounter I had that day stands out in my memory partly because of the location of our meeting, and partly because we had once shared so much in common. We had both grown up in similar circumstances and our social circles had overlapped. Our experiences of Hong Kong, and our connections to China, were also similar.

Yet here we were now having taken very different paths. In university I had taken a step towards political activism, standing up for the concerns we shared and fighting for a promise that mattered. As a student she had been recruited and trained by the pro-Beijing camp and was now a rising star in their circle. Our political paths mirrored each other's, and we both now found ourselves in the spotlight and in leadership roles.

The moment our eyes met that day I remembered the person I had known. She was very active in organizing extracurricular events and meeting new friends. She seemed an ambitious person who wanted to craft her image as a successful individual. That may be the reason why she stands for the opposite camp – a position where she can access enormous opportunity and wealth.

It would be easy to see in her actions that day someone struggling with their conscience. And yet, in a system that incentivizes us to set aside our conscience, to make what China likes to call 'pragmatic' decisions, I could very easily have been her. Our similar backgrounds meant we were exposed to the same efforts to shape our politics around the ideas of the CCP. We had been members of the same student organization, without knowing much about its background and aims when we joined. I saw it as a way to broaden my horizons and expand my social circle. I did not even think about its political inclination at the beginning – and I didn't have the intellectual capacity to identify it either. It branded itself as non-political and provided resources for participants to organize activities. Even so, we soon realized its underlying motives.

Besides recreational activities, we were asked to join lectures and classes as 'civil education'. At the time we went along with it without taking it too seriously, as some of what would be presented simply did not fit with what we saw happening in our own community. We were told only that the CCP had been good for China, that it had saved China from hardship and strife because of evil foreign powers, and that all of Hong Kong had rejoiced in the liberation from colonial oppression

in 1997. We were also taught to see the world as being in com-
petition with China, seeking to keep China down and
humiliate it. The problem was that this was simply not what
our own families either remembered or felt. The image of
China presented to us contradicted our direct experience.
Even so, it did frame the way we understood what was happening. For me and my friend, what mattered was the sense
of camaraderie we felt as part of the group and that it made us
feel rewarded – it incentivized us, both socially and materially, to simply go with the flow.

Only later would I discover that this organization, which
also provides extracurricular and recreational activities for
students and young people, is controlled by the CCP and part
of the United Front. All of the leadership were pro-Beijing
politicians. As well as shaping opinion and fostering loyalty,
it is also tasked with recruiting new blood for the pro-
establishment camp.

She had been identified and then enlisted by the authorities to go on to bigger things. I was not. But had I been
earmarked and approached like her, what would I have done?
It's difficult to tell as I was not as politically conscious then as
I am now. I was naive and undereducated about the nature of
the organization. I sometimes wonder why I wasn't picked.
What had those in authority seen in me that ruled me out?
Had I been less attentive than my friend, or viewed as lacking
the necessary leadership traits? Perhaps I didn't display the
loyalty and dedication they prized? Perhaps I was not 'pragmatic' enough to warrant an approach? Had they seen
rebellion beneath my quiet and shy exterior, or a stubborn-
ness about what was right and wrong?

And if I had been picked, what promises might they have made? What would my family have thought? Would they have placed security over principles? And would I, wanting to be a good son, have accepted, to do right by them?

It is known that pro-Beijing legislators entice political assistants with promises of well-paid government jobs. I have friends who received such offers when attending job interviews, and who then turned them down. 'How could I live with myself, or look my friends in the eye?' was how a friend explained her decision. But accepting such an offer can be transformative for the whole family, providing financial security and opening up a network of contacts among the city's commercial and business elite. Whereas the politics of democracy advocates for fairness and equality of opportunity, Hong Kong's pro-Beijing and supposedly pro-Communist establishment embrace cronyism in the name of making connections (*guanxi*).

Sitting in exile, cut off from my home and from a family I dare not even contact, it's easy to wonder whether the pragmatic choice might not have been the best. While I do ponder the choices I have made, the truth is that I do not regret taking the path I did. Some decisions may prove wrong in retrospect, but the decision to remain truthful to myself and what I know and believe in is a matter of principle. Choosing to embrace the principles of freedom and democracy is also a decision to stand by truth. The trouble is that for a lot of people the truth is getting murkier.

Society Torn Apart

Ever since beginning my undergraduate degree, I had devoted almost all my time and energy to activism. Living in the spotlight of the political unrest engulfing Hong Kong was both mentally and physically demanding. When the world is swirling around you, it is easy to get sucked into the storm. I felt burnt out and knew I needed a break.

At the end of 2018, before the breakout of the 2019 Anti-Extradition Movement,* I applied for graduate programmes at a number of universities. Some time away studying on a quiet campus was what I needed. It would be an opportunity to step back, but also to grow intellectually and to mature my thinking.

Even if I stepped back from activism, politics would never go away. Beijing would continue to interfere in Hong Kong, chipping away at our freedoms and undermining our identity. There seemed to be a steady stream of bad news, and though people did their best to remain upbeat, the mood on the street was depressed. It was impossible to remain in Hong Kong and not feel this way, nor feel the strong pull of my conscience to resist.

It is important to be honest with yourself, to acknowledge how you feel and also your own limitations. Political activism is not just about fighting every little battle that crosses your

---

* The Anti-Extradition Movement was a series of protests which began in reaction to plans to allow 'criminal suspects' to be extradited from Hong Kong to Mainland China.

path every day. It is about keeping sight of the goal and the direction you wish to take. It is about thinking strategically and for the long term. There is an expectation, from others and in ourselves, that you should step up and resist every act that unreasonably encroaches on the rights and freedoms of our peoples. There is a sense of needing to follow every development, of knowing all you can as it happens. But sometimes it is good to step back and focus on the bigger picture.

Preparing for my applications to further my studies abroad, I worked hard to ensure I could meet the academic and linguistic requirements and pass the required tests. I was lucky to be able to call on friends in academia who could advise me on schools and courses, and provide guidance on the application process and scholarships, as the costs of studying abroad were beyond what I could afford.

In March 2019 I received the good news that the Council on East Asian Studies had awarded me a full scholarship to study East Asian Studies at Yale University in the US. I felt both honoured and very privileged to be given this opportunity – Yale is not only a great university, it is also ideally situated. It is only a few hours by train to New York and Washington DC, where I had friends who were advocating for greater international awareness of what was happening in Hong Kong. As China under Xi Jinping became increasingly hard-line and authoritarian, this international effort began to take on more importance. From past visits I had the gut feeling that US political opinion on China was changing, and that this change mattered.

My supporters, colleagues and friends were all excited about the news and were happy for me. They knew I needed a break and understood that this was not me walking away, as the pro-Beijing press sought to frame it, but the distance I needed to recharge my spirit and better equip myself to continue the fight. It was also an incredible opportunity for me, as only a few years before I would never even have considered being able to study abroad, let alone at such a world-class university.

Shortly after I accepted the offer, a series of unexpected events forced me to rethink my plans. In June 2019, two months before I was booked to leave Hong Kong to begin my studies, the Anti-Extradition Movement exploded on to the scene, first in such numbers and then with such ferocity that it would catch the world's attention.

On 12 February 2019, the Hong Kong government proposed a Bill to amend the Fugitive Offenders Ordinance, so that anyone considered a fugitive from Mainland China, Taiwan and Macau was no longer safe in Hong Kong, regardless of the fact that the city doesn't have any extradition agreements with those jurisdictions. With support from the pro-establishment majority in the Legislative Council, the government was determined to push the amendment, despite concerns that it provided a means for people in Hong Kong to be extradited to Mainland China, where there is no rule of law and where torture, disappearances and forced confessions are commonplace.

While activists and concerned citizens staged a series of protests, public concerns were mounting. What was at stake struck at the very heart of the community: personal security. For a population comprising in large part of families who had once sought refuge in Hong Kong from the CCP, who had experienced the true meaning of Chinese law and who had lost family members to the predations of the CCP, this hit a raw nerve.

Though the Bill laid out conditions as to when a prisoner might be extradited, it was not lost on people that such provisions depended entirely on the ability of the Hong Kong government to stand up to China. It was simply inconceivable that a Hong Kong official would turn down a request from Beijing.

Only three years previously, Hong Kong had been shaken by the news that five people working at a Hong Kong bookshop who had disappeared the previous year had been kidnapped and were being held in detention incommunicado across the border. The Hong Kong authorities had not even been informed. Many civil society groups worried that pro-democracy activists would be targeted for extradition. The fear that this was possible would be enough to silence dissent. Indeed, the bookseller Lam Wing Kee, who was allowed to return to Hong Kong after making a forced confession, fled Hong Kong for Taiwan in April, fearing for his safety.

The Hong Kong government sought to justify the amendment of the law by referencing a murder case in which a Hong Kong man had travelled to Taiwan, killed his girlfriend there, then returned to Hong Kong. Hong Kong Chief Executive Carrie Lam spoke emotionally of feeling it was her responsibility to do right by the family of the murdered girl, and to do all she could to ensure that the murderer faced justice. The problem was, as I found out when I joined several Hong Kong legislators in Taiwan in May to raise the issue with Taiwanese officials, that the Hong Kong government had made no official approach towards its Taiwanese counterpart to see how the latter might assist. Besides, the Taiwanese government had made it very clear that there were other arrangements that might be made in this case that would allow for the suspect to be handed over. Nor did they welcome the proposed extradition Bill, which they considered would endanger Hong Kong residents, including Taiwanese citizens.

Months of controversy were followed by protests as the Hong Kong government refused to back down, and continued to insist that the extradition Bill was only about the Taiwan case. They denied that Beijing had anything to do with the move, and repeatedly sought to play down fears that the proposed amendment would allow extradition to China. The more the government insisted, the more obvious it became that this was about politics rather than justice. There was speculation that Mrs Lam had made this move to buy herself time from having to pass the National Security Law which Beijing demanded, and which she must have known would be unpalatable to the Hong Kong public.

By June, opposition had evolved into mass protests larger than any seen in Hong Kong. On 9 June, more than a million people took to the streets in peaceful protest, the first of three million-plus protests that summer. The protest made two simple demands: withdraw the Bill, and make government accountable. But the government refused to engage and simply continued as if nothing had happened, with the second reading of the Bill as scheduled on 12 June.

The following weekend, 16 June, an estimated 2 million

people of Hong Kong's 7.5 million residents protested in what was one of the largest rallies anywhere in the world. That is over a quarter of the population. It is likely that even more would have joined had it been physically possible, as Hong Kong's world-class transport system was tested to its capacity. Many protestors waited several hours for trains and buses, while others walked across town to reach the rallying point. This time the protestors expressed not only their opposition to the Bill, but also their growing anger at a government that was not only unaccountable, but also increasingly alien in its tone and attitude, and dismissive of the people it claimed to represent.

I was at almost every rally during the critical first two months. In June and July, I often found myself caught among a sea of humanity. There were people of every age, background and walk of life. Eminent lawyers walked beside market stall traders, grandparents beside their grandchildren. These were the very best of people, behaving with a calm dignity and respect for one another, marching in protest together. Often the protests consumed the whole weekend, as people left home early or even the day before to get closer to the starting point. A march that would usually have taken an hour would take an entire day as millions filed along the route.

I experienced the protest as both an organizer and a participant. I was one of the few invited on to the temporary stage to address the protestors, rallying the crowd and appealing for its support for an invigorated movement. I was also there at the end of the day, standing beside the minority of 'front-liners' in full protective gear – hard hats, goggles and

makeshift body armour – and carrying umbrellas and bottled
water to fend off tear gas as they confronted fully armed riot
police in tense stand-offs. At this point, the very beginning of
the months-long protests, the protestors did their best to
maintain restraint. A lack of political leadership would con-
spire with a dishonest narrative from Beijing to turn this
divide into a chasm of mutual hate, turning people against
each other as dictatorships often do. But when I looked across
the massed crowds, all I could see were people trying to show
respect for their fellow citizens in difficult circumstances.
Middle-class protestors often came to the rally site with a
large bag of food and drinks to distribute to the others for
free. Inside the Mass Transit Railway (MTR) station, which
was the major transportation hub for the first few months of
protest, coins and bills were put on top of ticket machines to
ensure that others could afford to travel. Buying tickets with
cash, rather than using your Octopus card, also meant you
could avoid being tracked by the government. People on the
street looked after each other unconditionally. When tear gas
canisters were shot into the crowd, front-line protestors
rushed to the canisters and tried to put them out with water
so that the gas would not choke others. They literally risked
their health to mitigate the harm these chemical weapons
could do to the rest of the crowd. They demonstrated the
beauty of humanity.

Predictably, having failed to win popular support, Beijing
and the Hong Kong authorities recast the peaceful protest as
a violent riot. A call to drop the Bill was recorded as 'anti-
China separatism'. Our anger and agency could only be
explained away by imagining the meddling of foreign 'black

hands'. Then, when frustration finally turned to use of force, Beijing declared the protest to be terrorism. Those who sought to moderate would be accused of inciting violence and persecuted.

If resisting in Hong Kong had left me drained, the lesson I drew from the summer of 2019 was that it could also be invigorating. I love Hong Kong. It was more than just a home, it was everything to me. When I am in Hong Kong, I cannot help but feel fully committed to making it the free, open and diverse place Hongkongers deserve. The 2019 protests and the leaderless movement that arose from them inspired me. Though I did not have a prominent role, simply being part of this community made me feel alive. Even when you are alone, everything you do feels part of a collective, as if a million people you do not know are behind you, willing you on. No matter how limited my personal contribution, I feel part of something far larger, making history but also being on the right side of it.

By August, the time had come for me to decide whether to board the plane for Yale. It was so difficult to leave Hong Kong at such a critical time, even temporarily. However, it had become increasingly clear that the need for international advocacy was growing. We had no faith in an administration that had forgotten how to speak, and which was accountable only to a nation that did not listen. Our hopes now lay not only in protesting on the streets, but also in generating international pressure to push for change. Outside Hong Kong I would be better positioned to help the movement, to explain to the world what was happening and to ensure my people had a voice. As circumstances change, so must the protest movement.

State-Launched Smear Campaigns

In August 2019, I announced that I was heading to the US for graduate studies, and that I would also be continuing to serve Hong Kong's pro-democracy protest movement by focusing on international advocacy while I was there. This prompted an immediate response from Beijing. Chinese state media immediately framed my decision as further evidence that I did not care about Hong Kong and was somehow in league with foreign powers; they sought to portray it as an act of treachery, and to undermine the credibility of my offer. We must remember that this is a state so sensitive that it actually censored images of Winnie the Pooh simply for his passing resemblance to the 'great leader'. (It is often forgotten that the controversial image, of Pooh and Tigger walking together as friends, was meant to represent friendship between Xi and Obama.)

The state's social media accounts began to seed conspiracies about me. I was accused of being anti-Chinese, and controlled by 'hostile foreign agents' to incite violence and promote separatism. In fact, I had never incited violence nor called for anything other than for China to honour its promises. To me, saying that my fellow citizens deserve the right to decide their own future is pretty clear evidence that I love my city. More than that, I want to see the Chinese people enjoy democratic rights to hold their government accountable while China opens up itself and becomes a respected member of the international community. Demanding reform does not mean betrayal. It could also be a sign of care. For making a distinction between China and the CCP, between a people and a party, and between a nation and a regime, I was accused of being anti-Chinese.

Beijing used my story to reframe the Hong Kong protests, a local and very Chinese grievance, as part of an international conspiracy against China. A narrative was pushed that what was happening in Hong Kong was a Colour Revolution fomented by the capitalist West. State media accused the West, and the US in particular – not President Trump, but American politicians and the American people – of having a 'Cold War mentality'. The message from Beijing was that the West had taken advantage of Hong Kong's economic and social inequality to open up a new front in a new Cold War against China, inciting young people to riot and thereby destroying the harmonious and prosperous society the CCP had done so much to create.

When the international press refused to follow this lead, reporting on Beijing's claims but also highlighting that these claims were unfounded and contradicted by the experience of their own reporters on the ground, they became part of the Western conspiracy. In China, where information is strictly controlled and divergent opinion heavily suppressed, but also to a degree in Hong Kong's pro-Beijing circles, this new narrative was remarkably successful.

In June a friend noted that in neighbouring Guangdong Province there had been murmurs of understanding for their Hong Kong neighbours, if not open support. People, rumours suggested, were at first reluctant to pick sides. Many Chinese, especially in Southern China, have personal connections in Hong Kong. Many also understand the nature of the CCP regime. Yet three months later, public opinion in China had become fervently hostile, and Hong Kong was a nationalist issue. Hongkongers abroad were being harassed and in some cases assaulted by nationalist Chinese people with the encouragement of Beijing. Tightening control of information, Beijing then created a narrative to inflame public opinion. The CCP made people take sides and presented them with only one choice.

The Chinese regime could not be more hypocritical. It seems to believe that Chinese people have no capacity for independent thought and action, that they are sheep that must be led. If the shepherd is not the CCP, it will be the West leading them astray. If the Party is good, all that is not the Party or does not follow the Party must be evil. There could be no greater insult against a people than to see them this way, and no greater obstacle to international respect, let alone co-operation, between states.

The campaign to smear me was vicious and relentless. In the course of a few weeks, millions of threads with hundreds of millions of views appeared online, in forums and on social media, each small lie compounding to portray me as compromised and discredited. What I experienced was not the dark side of freedom of expression. Indeed, as multiple research reports would later show, the Chinese state was actively establishing networks of fake automated accounts to spread disinformation on Hong Kong, not only within China but around the world.[*]

---

[*]   'Retweeting through the Great Firewall: A persistent and undeterred threat actor', https://www.aspi.org.au/report/retweeting-through-great-firewall; 'How China built a Twitter propaganda machine then let it loose on Coronavirus', https://www.propublica.org/article/how-china-built-a-twitter-propaganda-machine-then-let-it-loose-on-coronavirus

I had found myself a target of the 'Little Pink Warriors', China's army of online nationalists who are directed and incentivized to troll those deemed to be an enemy of China. This army swarmed all over my social media accounts, barraging me with abuse and threatening me and those around me. They left comments and spread disinformation on forums and in chat groups. Chinese communities in particular were targeted, as Beijing sought to mislead people and turn our own communities against us.

It was alleged that I had been trained by the CIA and was receiving payments from the US government to subvert China. It was also alleged that my family's ancestral hall in Shenzhen had been demolished and that I had lost hundreds of millions of renminbi, which was why I was revolting against the state. (In China, ancestral halls were destroyed by the Communists, who saw them as a symbol of 'Old China' which they wished to replace. However, as restrictions eased in the 1990s and into the 2000s, many families returned and donated money, often taking out loans, to rebuild their ancestral halls – which the CCP today parades as its own achievement.) Other trolls claimed that I had abandoned my friends and the Hong Kong people to live a life of luxury in the West. As absurd as these stories may seem, and as easy as each is to prove wrong, there were many people, not only in China but across the world, who believed them.

With the controlled media landscape in China, the stigmatization from the state could depict to millions of viewers a 'virtual' Nathan Law with a completely untrue personality, personal experiences and characteristics. This is appalling, and has incurred many consequences. While in the US I received numerous threats on my life. These I reported to the university and local authorities, who conducted their own investigation. I was assured that the threats were traced and those who had made them were known to the authorities. Even so, I couldn't help but feel insecure. I was particularly concerned that my location and private details were known to those threatening me. Knowing you are being watched, and that people wish you harm, is a terrible experience to live with. Even today I still worry, and must be alert. It is something you never get fully used to. I can only thank fortune that I have not yet been physically attacked, and that I have good friends around me. Friends and people I can trust.

Who Owns Truth?

Facts are objective. However, how such information is presented is subjective. This is a topic of much discussion in free societies. It is common to hear people talk of reading multiple news sources and of aiming to find the middle ground. However, it would be wrong to let such an understanding guide the way in which we engage with information from a closed, unaccountable and state-controlled environment, as exists in China.

In China, and increasingly in Hong Kong, what constitutes a 'fact' is not determined by what happened, but by what the political authorities *say* happened. When the facts no longer represent the truth, it is right to reject them. It is wrong to try to see 'both sides' where, on one side, the truth does not exist. And we must be very wary of those who seek to change the facts.

Take the horrific Yuen Long attacks on the evening of 21 July 2019, which we mentioned in Chapter 2. Yuen Long is a commuter town of around 200,000 people, situated in the New Territories close to Hong Kong's border with Mainland China. It is linked to the city by a public railway system, with Yuen Long station serving as a thoroughfare and hub for local transport links. During peak hours it is not unusual to see passengers packed tight, standing shoulder to shoulder.

As protestors joined commuters returning home by train after a day of peaceful protests, they were set upon as they exited the station concourse by a mob of white-shirted men all identically armed with wooden sticks. These men were members of local clan associations loyal to Beijing and with a history of organized violent crime, including triad links. The mob had gathered earlier in the day, and had even been addressed by Junius Ho, a leading pro-Beijing lawmaker. It was also known that Beijing officials had recently had direct contact with the clan heads.

At least forty-five people were badly injured in the attacks, including the elderly and young children. Despite thousands of calls made to the police emergency hotline and people streaming into the local police station seeking help, the police response was at best hesitant. It was thirty-nine minutes after the first emergency call was received that the police entered the station in force, long after the assailants had already left. Despite the assailants being armed and remaining outside the station, and there being many witnesses to the attacks, the police made no arrests on the site.

Matthew Cheung, Hong Kong's Chief Secretary of Administration, was severely reprimanded for simply stating the obvious: that the Hong Kong Police Force's response had not met public expectations. Despite receiving an avalanche of complaints, the police refused calls for an independent investigation, agreeing only to an internal investigation by its own Independent Police Complaints Council (IPCC) – a body controlled by pro-Beijing figures. Unsurprisingly, the IPCC ruled the incident to be a 'gang fight', implying that responsibility for the event also lay with the victims.

Chief Executive Carrie Lam and the Hong Kong government, while condemning the attacks, sought to focus attention away from what had happened and towards a fringe pro-democracy protest that same evening outside China's Liaison Office that had seen protestors throw paint at the Chinese national emblem. Although no one had been hurt, she framed the security concerns felt by Hong Kong residents who had just witnessed an unprovoked attack on ordinary residents in a commuter train station as if it were the result of a fear of protestors. Condemning the fringe protests as a riot, the government refused to apply the same label to what had happened in Yuen Long.

The incident was soon taken up by Radio Television Hong Kong (RTHK). Based on the British BBC, it is independent and had a well-deserved reputation for impartiality, operating to the highest journalistic standards before its leadership reshuffle in 2021. RTHK commissioned one of its most respected producers, Bao Choy, to investigate what had happened in Yuen Long that day. On 30 October 2020, a year after the event, it was broadcast as an episode of *Hong Kong*

Connection (akin to BBC's *Panorama*), entitled '7.21 – Who Owns the Truth?'.

The documentary showed that by 6 p.m., four and a half hours before the attack at Yuen Long station, groups of masked men in white shirts and armed with sticks had already gathered and were loitering around the town centre. Many were carrying the Chinese flag. There were already reports of these men attacking people seemingly at random and striking passers-by with their sticks. The police, while aware of the situation, sought neither to confront these groups nor to disperse them. One of those attacked, whose ordeal was pieced together by the investigating journalists, was a young chef who had just come off his work shift in a nearby mall. He was chased by several of the armed men and savagely beaten. He sustained serious injuries and was hospitalized. There is no indication that he had provoked the mob.

The programme also showed that there were in fact two attacks in the station: the first at around 10.30 p.m., and the second at about midnight, after the police had left. There were also further attacks on people in the surrounding neighbourhood.

The story directly contradicted many of the key allegations made by the Hong Kong government and by the police. There was no indication of this being a fight between two similarly armed gangs. In fact, it was unclear why the victims were being targeted and beaten. Many of those attacked were evidently not protestors but simply commuters returning home. Police claims that no arrests were made because they 'saw no one holding weapons' were shown to be untruthful as images emerged of police officers standing alongside armed white-shirted men.

The authorities' attempt to blame the violence on protestors led by the democratic lawmaker Lam Cheuk-ting were also shown up by the evidence. Lam, a veteran politician, is a former investigator for the police's own anti-corruption watchdog, the Independent Commission Against Corruption (ICAC), and is known to be a calm and moderating presence in the legislature. Video evidence proved that Lam arrived in Yuen Long long after the attacks had already started, and intervened only to attempt to defuse the situation. Despite this, on 26 August 2020 the government arrested Lam for 'rioting'.

Most damaging for the authorities was video footage showing police officers fraternizing with the mob immediately after the attacks. Unsurprisingly, many speculated that the police had colluded with organized crime groups, and that the clan 'bosses' had been informed that the police wouldn't intervene in their actions. It is not uncommon for police officers to be recruited from families with clan connections, for one brother to join the police and another to be initiated into a triad organization. The clans, who hold no ideological loyalty, have a history of working with the CCP, and it has not gone unnoticed that in the previous few years, and especially since the rise of Xi Jinping, the clans and triads are again operating as political tools. From the case of Kevin Lau, a former editor of the newspaper *Ming Pao*, who was jumped and repeatedly stabbed in broad daylight in the middle of the city as he was getting out of his car, to the sudden deployment of Yuen Long clan members (yes, them again) to rough up pro-democracy protestors in Mong Kok during the 2014 protest, the writing was on the wall.

The Yuen Long station attack broke the already limited trust many people had in the government and the police. The authorities were seen not just as dishonest, but as fundamentally bad. They no longer seemed able even to acknowledge reasonable and sincerely held concerns. They stuck by Beijing's narrative even when the facts showed it to be absurd. It was not lost on many that the attacks on Yuen Long met the criteria for terrorism. When people are respected, trust is built on transparency and accountability. When people are not, the facts are something you are told and trust is simply demanded of you.

Bao Choy's investigative work was received with critical praise within journalistic circles, and her documentary '7.21 – Who Owns the Truth?' was awarded the prestigious Kam Yiu-yu Press Freedom Award. However, on 3 November 2020, four days after the programme was first aired, Bao was arrested; in April 2021 she became the first person to be sentenced in relation to the Yuen Long attack.

Threatened with closure, RTHK is being reformed for the new Hong Kong. Its head has been replaced with a government bureaucrat. Several programmes and commentators that were even mildly critical of the government have been axed, including the long-running satirical show *Headliner*; and episodes of other programmes have been pulled from the air at short notice for political reasons. Carrie Lam now has her own show that airs four times a day, every day of the week.

Even now, the Hong Kong Police claim that the Yuen Long incident was a 'balanced fight between two groups' instigated by pro-democracy protestors. The police response time has been corrected, from thirty-nine minutes to eighteen minutes.

Any account that disputes this is deemed to be 'fake news' and the result of malign foreign interference.

Lies rarely work immediately. What they do is muddy the water. Today in Hong Kong, despite overwhelming evidence from credible sources, there is confusion as to what happened in Yuen Long and, as in so many things, the public are deeply divided.

There are those who remember what happened. Those who witnessed events as they unfolded on their screens as unfiltered images of the attacks were streamed live. Among journalists and civil society groups, whose job it was to report objectively and come to the aid of those affected, memories are still fresh. Whether we read the *New York Times* or the *Wall Street Journal*, the *Guardian* or the *Telegraph*, or get our news from Al Jazeera, Deutsche Welle or France 24, the story is the same.

Then there are those, a vocal and influential minority, who listen to what Beijing tells them. They accept the narrative that says the attacks were between two evenly matched armed groups of loyal local patriots and violent pro-democracy pro-testors. They will say the violence was the fault of a democratic legislator. They will wish away the inconvenient truths, and cling instead to unfounded conspiracies that confirm their prejudices.

It is never easy to ascertain the truth. The facts are important, but we must not take them for granted. We need to know our source; to be critical and not simply believe; to develop our ability to distinguish between a difference of perspective and an outright lie. It is no good simply accepting the middle ground. We must never be afraid to stand resolutely on the side of what is true, and to speak the truth.

The more tribal the information space becomes, whether on social media or in our politics, the less critical we are. The truth has never been more important. Never has free, honest and accountable journalism been more important, but also our ability to know our sources. Authoritarian regimes, and those who refuse to respect us as citizens while demanding our loyalty as subjects, benefit from our ignorance, prejudices and also our desire not to cause offence. They rise as civil society weakens and our confidence in journalism falls. They exploit our divisions and our desire to have simple answers. And, like cults and conspiracy theorists, they prey on our own blindness to entice us into a reality that they control, where black turns to white at their command.

Truth with 'Chinese Characteristics'

In the dictionary of authoritarianism, anything embellished as having 'Chinese characteristics' is apt to be redefined to suit the CCP. The meaning might be completely different, even contradictory. It doesn't need to be reasonable or even to make any sense. After all, the idea of what is reasonable and what makes sense can also be given 'Chinese characteristics'. Thus China's disputes, including those arising from its encroachment into areas internationally recognized as being beyond its borders, whether in India or Bhutan or in the South China Sea, are presented by Beijing as 'indisputable'. Similarly, while China expects to control the global narrative and discourse about itself, makes the most forceful demands of others not to recognize Taiwan, and openly operates a United Front department to co-ordinate efforts overseas, it presents itself as non-interfering. And so we have the contradictions of modern China.

The CCP controls the internet, media and increasingly the social information space in China. It has developed its own ecosystem, with Chinese companies and service providers that conform to and work with the Chinese state. Not only is nothing private but, should the Party wish, everything is controllable. Private messages, comments and forums may be deleted. Companies or products can be removed from search engines. Even online shopping portals must bend to the regime's will if it is politically expedient. Such a concentration of the power to shape what people see, know and are able to discuss allows the CCP to mould public opinion in a way that's inconceivable in a free and open society.

China's closed system of information allows for words and concepts to take on meanings that are detached from how they are commonly understood in the rest of the world. This is because the CCP's definition of a term cannot be publicly challenged, nor are people in China exposed to the open exchange of ideas that shapes meaning and understanding in open societies.

An attempt to engage a Chinese audience in open (albeit moderated) discussion on subjects including Hong Kong and Taiwan, and to interact with ordinary Hongkongers and Taiwanese people directly, was tried in early 2020 through Clubhouse, a new open-forum-style app. Ordinary Chinese citizens set up and tuned in to a host of forums with other Chinese people around the world. The discussions showed the gulf in understanding between people living in a closed system where information is strictly controlled and those free to find out the truth, but also that within China there are many people who wish to connect with others to form a better understanding. What better way to 'promote friendship' between Chinese people, and to contribute to the 'peace and prosperity of our global village', to borrow the CCP's language. Yet within days of launching, and despite there being no incident that might conceivably represent a threat to the CCP, access to the app was banned in China. This came as no surprise to anyone. The issue is not what was said, but that the CCP was unable to control what Chinese people heard.

In China, the news is not there to inform. As with everything, it must first and foremost serve the Party. What passes as discussion is effectively staged, as all voices are channelled through state-monitored sources. The role of such controlled information is simply to define the thoughts of Chinese citizens, to promote unquestioning loyalty and obedience to the Party, which in turn secures the Party's monopoly rule.

The trouble with authoritarian regimes is that by their very nature they lack the legitimacy which comes with accountability and a means for the ordered transfer of power. Without an opposition and a mature civil society, there is no corrective to the regime when it does wrong; without that, there is no justice. The more authoritarian a system, the more important the veneer of legitimacy becomes.

In 2013 President Xi launched a massive publicity campaign across China to promote what the CCP calls the twelve Core Socialist Values (CSVs). These are: for the nation, prosperity, democracy, civility and harmony; for society, freedom, equality, justice and rule of law; and for the individual, patriotism, dedication, integrity and geniality. These all sound admirable. The trouble is not what is written – China's constitution too is an admirable document – but how the CCP chooses to understand and apply (or not apply) these values. After all, the mafia doesn't say they trade in murder and extortion; they say they value loyalty and respect.

My activism and my politics are defined not only by believing in a particular kind of liberal democracy, but also because I recognize and reject authoritarianism and the very real oppression that exists in my home country. While I respect the sensitivities of many progressives in the West, towards revisionism, micro-aggressions and historic wrongs, these feel to me like the problems of a society that has already addressed the larger and more absolute oppression that exists in China. My family was raised to expect levels of corruption, injustice and inequality that simply do not exist in the more developed and liberal countries: they know that the authorities tell outright lies, and disappear and torture people who simply challenge what the regime says is true. Chinese people are raised, within the cultural and societal landscape shaped by the dominant CCP, to tolerate great injustices, and to focus simply on keeping their heads down and working hard.

The contradictions of the PRC are not lost on the people of Hong Kong. The regime protects ethnic minorities' rights on paper, yet cultural genocide is state policy; freedom of religion is guaranteed by the constitution, yet religions are state-sanctioned and controlled. Even religious texts, including the

Bible and the Quran, are rewritten to be in line with CCP doctrine.*

In a well-known passage of the Bible (John 8:7), an adulterous woman is brought before Jesus, and her accusers ask if she should be killed by stoning for her sins. In every authentically translated version of scripture, Jesus responds, 'Let him who is without sin among you be the first to throw a stone at her.' These words disperse the angry crowd, and Jesus tells the woman, 'Go, and from now on sin no more.'

In the CCP telling the crowd leaves, but Jesus tells the woman, 'I too am a sinner. But if the law could only be executed by men without blemish, the law would be dead.' Then Jesus proceeds to stone the woman to death. That this retelling distorts the original message, which is of forgiveness, may seem not only wrong but offensive to many Christians. It is, however, the only version of the story China's reported 100 million Christians will be allowed to learn. What the CCP wants people to learn is that the law must be obeyed without question, because in China the law is whatever the CCP says.†

No one would disagree with the twelve Core Socialist Values as they are written. In fact, these are all values that drive the protests in Hong Kong. We believe that for there to be prosperity, civility and harmony in the nation there must be genuine accountability through democracy; and that for a

---

* 'The gospel according to Xi', https://www.wsj.com/articles/the-gospel-according-to-xi-11591310956

† 'China To Christians: We're Rewriting The Bible, And You'll Use It Or Else', https://www.frc.org/op-eds/china-to-christians-were-rewriting-the-bible-and-youll-use-it-or-else

society to be free, just and equal there must be rule of law. We believe in dedication, integrity and geniality – all of which were on display in the mass protests of 2014 and 2019.

The problem is that for Beijing, each of these values holds a different meaning. Prosperity need not include everyone. Civility and harmony mean there should be no criticism nor dissent. Democracy is a one-party system where the National People's Congress must applaud, vote and speak on command. The rule of law is a political tool with which to deny the separation of powers, the presumption of innocence and the right of habeas corpus, to disappear persons, to accept torture and forced confessions, and to operate a system of hired thugs and unofficial so-called 'black jails'.

According to its stated values, Beijing cares about freedom. Freedom from what? Freedom to do what? Freedom to accept the state into every part of our lives. Freedom from knowing the truth. The state controls where we can live or travel. The state watches and controls all information. It is the freedom of having a social credit system to reward and punish us for all we do, and to demand that private companies share everything with the authorities, regardless of confidentiality. This 'free' country spends more on 'internal security' than it does on defence, and in dealing with the COVID-19 outbreak had no qualms about physically locking people into their homes.

These Core Socialist Values are about ideological discipline, taking up Stalin's call to 'engineer the soul'. For Xi, ideological discipline is a means to further consolidate power. What people in Hong Kong and around the world celebrated about China's rise in the past forty years, since Deng

Xiaoping began opening China to the world, Xi sees as a threat. It was hoped that economic development and China's greater integration into the global order would open the door to more freedoms and new ideas. Xi is determined to ensure this never happens.

Communiqué Number 9 spells this out. It instructs Party and government officials to 'wage intense struggle' against Western constitutional democracy and the ideas of impartial journalism, universal human rights, civil society and 'historical nihilism' (meaning the promotion of history detached from CCP ideology – or what Xi Jinping determines to be history).* Chinese democracy (*minzhu*) rejects what China dismissively calls a voting democracy – you might be forgiven for thinking there was only one kind, but China considers itself a Party-internalized 'working' democracy. At the same time, the communiqué not only rejects human rights, civil society, a free and independent press and access to information, but sees them as an enemy. 'Universal suffrage', as the CCP sought to implement it in Hong Kong, means that people can vote, but only for candidates of the Party's choosing. This is selection, not election.

The Core Socialist Values are not a statement of the values guiding China at all. Instead, they co-opt the language of these values to provide the cultural and moral basis for a new model Chinese citizen. It is classic propaganda: using the language of democracy to undermine those ideals and overwrite the possibility of an alternative.

---

* 'Xi's China Is Steamrolling Its Own History', https://foreignpolicy.com/
2019/01/29/xis-china-is-steamrolling-its-own-history

Betraying Our Values

In late 2019 and early 2020, I was privileged to be invited on a speaking tour of several East Coast universities. At each university there were Chinese nationalists who protested my presence. I value the right to protest – for me, it's the mark of a free society. I also welcome the opportunity to engage with ideas, and to talk things through with people who have been misinformed. However, what did come as a surprise and a disappointment was not that these protestors disputed what I had to say, but that they sought to prevent me from saying anything at all.

Before my talk held in November 2019, the University of Pennsylvania received a letter from their Chinese Alumni Association demanding that I be disinvited from speaking there and my talk cancelled. The reason given was that it might harm relationships with China. While the university did not act on this, there were certainly those who supported the association's position. Consider for a moment what was being demanded, not as a favour but as a matter of course, by alumni of a US university: that a student legally studying in the US should not be allowed to travel to another US university to speak to US students.

At Johns Hopkins University, where I was joined by my friend Joshua Wong speaking from Hong Kong, there were dozens of protestors at the venue itself. The protesting students, all of whom were Chinese, were clearly organized, though they accounted for less than half of the Chinese students attending. Each had leaflets, and many carried identical banners. Having failed to deplatform us, the protestors attempted to shut down discussion at the venue itself by being disruptive and asking misleading questions. For example, in the questions asked, they portrayed the Hong Kong protest as a chaotic and destructive riot that attacked innocent people randomly. Some Chinese students equated themselves to Jews in the Second World War, to show that they were being targeted and suppressed in the 2019 protest movements. These are utterly wrong descriptions and comparisons that neglect basic facts and power relations. (The event, as it happens, was widely reported on by Chinese state media.)

I welcome questions, and the opportunity to confront the many lies spread by the Chinese authorities about Hong Kong and the Hong Kong protests. A common assertion, often posed as a question, was that the protestors are separatists or that we are being used and supported by the US government. There is a simple reply to this charge: none of the protest demands express subversive intent. Joshua and I have only ever asked for the principle of self-determination to be respected. How is it subversive, separatist or anti-China simply to say that Beijing should honour its agreement with Britain and the Hong Kong people, and that Hongkongers deserve a voice? As for being US agents who concocted the protest movement in league with the US government, if there was any credibility to such conspiracies, you would think the army of international journalists that descended on Hong Kong over the last few years would have reported on it. The reason no reputable media organization has done so is because there simply is no evidence – because it is not true.

There is no foreign 'black hand' orchestrating the protests.

What there is, however, is well-documented evidence, including in peer-reviewed academic papers, of interference from the CCP. This includes a global disinformation campaign that sought to reframe the protests as being foreign-orchestrated and violent, and the mobilization of organized criminal gangs who received payments and incentives to act as provocateurs and defame protestors. It is also well documented that the line on 'separatism' and 'foreign interference' conforms to a well-used CCP playbook, as is the deliberate entrenching of divisions by demonizing the perceived enemy.

Most of those seeking to silence me and others from speaking up about the Hong Kong protest movement are, understandably, from Mainland China. Despite receiving threats, my feelings towards them are overwhelmingly of sorrow and sympathy. This comes from a place of understanding, because I know personally through friends and family why they react in the way they do. The CCP has created in China a controlled information environment that conditions people to see and think in a particular way. And since Xi Jinping took power, it has only got worse.

When you are raised to believe the West is your enemy, and that people alone have no agency, the narrative of 'foreign interference' in Hong Kong may seem more plausible than the reality. Everywhere you turn, you are told about the 'feelings of the Chinese people' (as defined by the CCP). You are conditioned to feel and respond in a certain way, which serves the political interests of the CCP. The protests are just wrong because they are made to *feel* wrong.

News of Chloé Zhao winning the Oscar for Best Director in 2021 was not reported in China. Zhao is hardly a dissident.

Her crime was simply to let slip, in one interview eight years previously, her thoughts on being raised in China, and to speak a truth that most Chinese know in their hearts to be true. In 2012 the author Mo Yan was celebrated across China and the world as the first Chinese writer to win the Nobel Prize. Conveniently forgotten was Gao Xingjian, who won the same prize twelve years earlier. Gao, who was once part of the CCP's intellectual establishment and widely acclaimed in China, dared to reflect in his writings the thoughts of so many Chinese people following the Tiananmen Square Massacre. Today he is forgotten, his works banned.

My biggest surprise and source of disappointment has been that a minority of those who, despite living in a free society, choose simply not to believe the overwhelming evidence of what is reported in the free press and to align themselves with the CCP narrative. What is upsetting is not that they don't share my views, but that they have sought to shut me down and to deplatform me while claiming to share my values.

It is curious to see nationalist Chinese who seek to deny Hongkongers their most fundamental rights and who oppose the pursuit of freedom and democracy joined in solidarity by people in the West who claim to be anti-imperial, pro-human rights and to identify with progressive and democratic values. Ethno-nationalist chants of 'Hong Kong is China' and 'You are Chinese' are not exactly subtle, especially when delivered in Putonghua.

While I recognize that the majority of people who identify with the political Left do support Hong Kong, the reality is that there is a small minority who do not. Some are simply ignorant of China and are more focused on the shortcomings of their own societies and political systems. Others seem motivated less by values, which we might share, than by hate. Either way, what concerns me is how blind such people are to the basic realities of life in Hong Kong and in China.

I believe a better future to be one that is more just, fair and equitable. But I also understand that only with the accountability and choice that comes with democracy are these things possible. Only with the rule of law and a truly representative legislature can power be held to account and people feel safe. But I also understand that China is neither just, nor fair, nor equal, and that it is 'Communist' in its system of political authoritarianism only.

Politics is not a game. Nor is political activism. It is the last resort of a people who have no voice, no power and no means of being heard. There is something absurd about telling someone who has been politically persecuted, whose friends have been jailed, beaten and tortured, whose family have been threatened and who has had to flee his home seeking political asylum, that the situation in the US or UK is no better. This is not only simply untrue, it is also offensive and dangerous.

No system is perfect, no society completely fair. What matters is that people are free to engage with those who hold power in order to make things better. For all the faults that exist in the US, the UK or in other democratic states, this freedom exists and there are avenues open to us to express how we really feel. We are free to learn about the world, and to follow our conscience. We can speak the truth. It is important to remember that such freedoms are beyond what many people can enjoy.

The threat to our freedoms and all that we cherish comes not only from without, but also from within – from the bigotry that blinds us to understanding reality as it really is and from self-righteous moralizing at the expense of the truth. Good intentions do not make the silencing of others with whom we disagree right, nor is prejudice excused in the fight against the prejudice of others. When we reject the truth as reported by a free and independent press, attack the rule of law and silence a community, it does not matter if this is done in the name of patriotism, socialism or social justice: we erode the foundations of our freedoms and of our dignity. We must see the challenges we face from the expansion of authoritarianism as both global and urgent. We must understand this as an existential threat to living with dignity.

Silencing people is what authoritarians do. We should take inspiration from being challenged, and find insight in new points of view. My hope is that whoever is reading this can look beyond politics and recognize the common principles that allow us to live without fear, and to imagine a better future – a belief in democracy, self-determination and human rights. We should not let tribalized or partisan politics blind us to those who would undermine these values.

As George Orwell argued, in a time of universal deceit, telling the truth is a revolutionary act.

CHAPTER 6

BELIEVING IN THE POWER OF CHANGE

On 17 November 1989, eight days after the fall of the Berlin Wall, students gathered in Prague to protest against the Soviet regime that had held power in Czechoslovakia since 1946. More than 50,000 people took to the streets in what was the biggest anti-government protest in Czechoslovakia for twenty years. The authorities were determined to suppress it. The police, who had initially been ordered to hold back, were unleashed as the column of peaceful protestors marched on Wenceslas Square. A hundred and fifty people were arrested, and hundreds beaten.

The protests that day were the culmination of long-pent-up resentment against a regime that had stripped the people of their fundamental freedoms and dignity. But it was also the beginning of positive change, and the start of what would become known as the Velvet Revolution. At its height, over 200,000 people in Prague marched in protest. They were joined by similar protests across the country. What people demanded, and were prepared to risk so much to achieve, were free elections and the right to live in a free and open society – things so easily overlooked and taken for granted by those who already enjoy them.

On 29 December 1989, the one-party dictatorship of the Communist Party of Czechoslovakia ended. It was, as revolutions go, a relatively smooth and bloodless affair, and the start of a wave of democratization across what had been the Soviet Union, replacing totalitarian states with nations of people.

With the restoration of parliamentary democracy and free elections, the people of Czechoslovakia could once again enjoy those civil and political rights denied to them for forty-four years. Back in 1946, when the last free and fair election took place, people had voted into power a Communist Party they thought could better represent them. Few would have imagined that for many this vote would also be their last. Democracy was murdered through the ballot box. It would take a generation, and cost countless lives, to right this wrong and to mend their country.

Today, as I write this book in exile in London, having recently been granted political asylum by the UK government, I see many parallels between what happened in Czechoslovakia after the Second World War and what is now happening in Hong Kong. I am not alone in seeing this. Many Hongkongers, both in Hong Kong and around the world, see their home going through a similar process. It is a heart-rending experience. And, like so many others who have seen their home slowly fall into authoritarianism, I wonder if and when it might once again be free.

Before Beijing revealed its plan to overhaul Hong Kong's

electoral system, Hong Kong's elections were at least procedurally democratic. Politics did not preclude people from standing for election before 2016, or from voting. Voter anonymity was guaranteed. Of course, the system was designed so that even though the pro-democracy camp consistently won the popular vote, it was the pro-Beijing camp that held the majority of Legco seats, and 'selected' the Chief Executive and those appointed to the advisory Executive Council. In the 2016 election that I contested, pro-democracy parties took 55 per cent of the popular vote. Parties collaborated and strategic voting was encouraged. And yet pro-democracy candidates won only twenty-nine of the seventy seats.

At the time of writing, the last election in Hong Kong was two years ago, in November 2019. It was a District Council election. District councillors have limited and local powers. They have no legislative power. The District Councils are mandated to advise the government on local and community affairs without the authority to influence and participate directly in policy and budget formation. It was nevertheless an important election, coming as it did at the height of the 2019 protest. By that time, the overwhelming narrative being pushed by the government and by local papers beholden to Beijing was that public opinion was firmly in favour of 'patriots' – that a frustrated people, shocked by the mounting levels of violence, wanted an end to the protests. The pro-Beijing camp expected that these elections would vindicate this narrative. The District Councils had, after all, been a bastion of pro-Beijing support, ably assisted by community associations linked to the CCP's United Front. Never a priority for the pan-democratic camps, whose focus has been on

the legislative rather than district level, the councils have tra-
ditionally voted heavily for pro-Beijing candidates.

The District Council elections in November 2019 had a
turnout rate of 71 per cent, the highest in Hong Kong's history. Pro-democracy (and pro-protest) candidates won 388
out of 479 seats, and carried seventeen out of eighteen dis-
tricts. It was a stunning rebuke to the official narrative. Even
if those elected would be powerless to press the issues on
which people had cast their vote – even if the possibility of
change seemed so hopeless – there is power in signalling.
And this was a signal.

On 11 March 2021, the National People's Congress passed
a resolution for sweeping reforms of Hong Kong's electoral
system. The Election Committee was expanded to further
dilute the influence of the pro-democracy figures selected
through elected committees. The number of seats in the
Legislative Council was increased from seventy to ninety,
while those popularly elected were reduced from thirty-five
to twenty.

Since 1997, Beijing has controlled Hong Kong's political
system. What it demanded now was not only power, but the
elimination of an opposition. A vetting process was implemented to ensure that only 'patriots' approved by the
authorities would be allowed to contest an election.

This is done by the National Security Bureau, a newly
established and overtly political police department that
reports not to the Hong Kong government but to Beijing. Any
'suspect candidate' is barred, no evidence required. There is
no legal way to challenge a decision. No longer content with
tipping the power balance in Hong Kong politics, Beijing now

wants to control not only the outcome of elections, but the political discourse itself. It is worth reiterating that Beijing sees no contradiction in doing this while supposedly guaranteeing Hong Kong's promised political autonomy and way of life.

These reforms, which the authorities present as 'improving' Hong Kong's political system, have effectively put an end to any meaningful elections in Hong Kong. Until the CCP has been able to shape the people in its image in the city, candidates who command genuine popular support will be barred from running. Like those who voted in the Czechoslovakian elections in 1946, Hongkongers who voted in the 2016 Legislative Council and 2019 District Council elections were unaware that they were casting the last meaningful ballot before the regime crumbled.

Everything Is Fine, Until It Is Not

As I am writing this with my friend Evan Fowler, I am in an apartment in London. It is small and sparsely furnished. Building a home takes time, as does putting down roots. I chose to work on a mechanical keyboard, the type I used at my home in Hong Kong. The clicking sound made by each key as I type is comforting. When you lose your home, such small things matter. I decided to write this book with Evan because, although we may seem very different and come from different backgrounds, we are both Hongkongers and we both feel very deeply for our home. It is not politics that draws people like us to speak up, but our love for our home and our people. Our activism comes from conscience.

Evan would not like me describing him as an activist. In many ways he does not fit the mould. He is slightly embarrassed by public protest. He doesn't enjoy crowds. But activism has many guises and takes many forms – and in his own way, through quiet conversation, he is as much a part of our movement as anyone else. I asked him to work with me on this book because in our differences lies an important lesson: that movements that matter are not partisan, but reach across political and cultural distinctions. Activism is a broad church. We should be defined not by our divisions but by our shared ideals.

Neither Evan nor I grew up hating the CCP. To be completely frank, we did not care. What we care about is the relationships we have with the people around us, with our community and our home. To defend what is important to us, and to stand firm for the values we believe in, does not and should not rely on hatred of the opposition. But if two peoples grow apart, as with any relationship, we should ask why. Just as one person should never be owned by another, one group of people cannot be the property of another. Relationships are not imposed.

Like me, Evan is unlikely to return home. Public association with me carries a risk, and the National Security Law applies globally. As the case of *Apple Daily* showed, these days even to pen an op-ed leaves one open to arrest. It is sobering to remember that the Hong Kong government cannot guarantee that it will not arrest people for merely reading 'offending' material. Both of us are haunted by a home, by friends and by family, we accept we may not see again.

I remember vividly the time, in March 2020, when I returned to Hong Kong during my studies at Yale. It meant so much to me personally to be in my homeland and among my people at such a critical time. I was driven by a passionate need to stand shoulder to shoulder with my comrades on the street, to continue my advocacy work, and to begin campaigning for the 2020 Legislative Council elections that were meant to take place. Everyone knew these elections were important. While, predictably, the authorities were finding excuses to postpone these elections, no one expected to see Beijing take such a hard line with the National Security Law. When I stood in solidarity with protestors and lent my voice to the chorus of our leaderless protest movement, I never truly imagined that these actions would lead me into a life of exile, far from this vibrant yet tortured city I love so much. Nonetheless, this is how things stand.

I remember the last time I wished my mum goodnight. Her face was calm yet loving, as it always seems to be. Her head lay on her pillow. I remember the sense of comfort and security around her. She did not know I was leaving. I could not tell her. She would have known I might have to leave sometime – she understood China, and China is a place where there is much that must not be said. I miss her. And I miss being able to speak with her freely. If she reads this book, I would like her to know how much I love her, and how much family means to me. Her love was the greatest gift any mother can give, as it taught me to love and be sensitive to the condition of others. It is also why, in trying times, I have not been able to take the more pragmatic path she had wanted me to. I know this has disappointed her, but I hope she understands.

I miss Hong Kong. I miss my two rescue cats, Papa and Fourteen, and the soft feel of their bodies on my hand as I stroked and played with them. I miss taking public transport with all the other Hongkongers who rely on it to get around. The subway, the MTR, with its tiled stations and slick, clean trains, opened up the city for development and has defined commuter life for the majority of working people (though in the latter stages of the 2019 protests, the MTR became notorious among protestors and activists for assisting the government in its crackdown). Then there are the buses, air-conditioned to feel freezing outside of rush hour; and, on those occasions when time matters more than money, the smell of sweat and the feel of faux leather in Hong Kong's ubiquitous red taxis. In Hong Kong I never thought of needing to drive. Today I am learning.

What I miss most about my home is its spirit. It is the constant buzz of a community always on the go. Of a people free with their words. It is the sound of Cantonese being spoken, of traffic horns and of the clatter of a million footsteps racing from one place to the next.

London is undoubtedly an amazing city, and I am grateful now to live here. It is a city that in so many ways offers much more than Hong Kong ever could. But if in London's internationalism I find much that can remind me of home, it is also this internationalism that sets London apart for me. The Hong Kong to which I belonged was the local city, united less by our multicultural history than by a shared language and lived experience. It was not the Hong Kong of the wealthy or the international set. It was the Hong Kong of the common people. These were my people, and my community, and I miss them.

I am still learning to rewire the experiences I had before I departed Hong Kong in June 2021. All those little moments, so negligible in daily life, have become so precious to me. Memory matters, and rather than wallow in misfortune we should embrace each experience and find in it the means to grow stronger and better as a person. As the poet David Whyte wrote, 'We learn, grow and become compassionate and generous as much through exile as homecoming, as much through loss as gain, as much through giving things away as in receiving what we believe to be our due.'

Exile is more than a geographical concept. We can be exiled from our home if the home we know is no longer allowed to be. It is a sense of deprivation many people in Hong Kong feel, and they are not alone in feeling this way. As the CCP seeks to shape China as an ethno-nationalist state dominated by the Han people, those who do not conform to the Party's narrative and who have experienced a very different history are increasingly being 'harmonized'. In Xinjiang, as has been well documented, but also in Tibet, Inner Mongolia and in other non-Han areas of China, what is happening is far worse.

What has happened in Hong Kong and elsewhere in China did not occur overnight. The signs were there. The foundations were laid in the co-opting of business interests, the elites and the media. Many noted the subtle revisions of history and of what we were asked to remember, the changing expectations of what it means to be Chinese. And yet the speed of deterioration has been much faster than anyone thought.

Today, Xi Jinping's China seeks to define international norms and standards, and the global discourse. This is not limited to our understanding of China; it also concerns how we understand our freedoms relative to autocracy. Across the world our business and elites – often, too, our political elites – have been co-opted. Journalism is being challenged, as is our trust in those institutions on which an open and free society is founded. To make the world safe for the CCP it demands control. Hong Kong, Beijing continues to insist, is a free and open society – and China, according to the CCP, is the most successful democracy in the world. We all know these are lies, but they are repeated in the hope that familiarity will deaden our resolve to correct them.

Xinjiang shows how far Beijing is prepared to go to crush dissent and assimilate a people. Hong Kong shows how Beijing is able to do this in a society that was once free and open, and under the international spotlight. It is imperative that we do not overlook the power we have in a liberal and democratic society, not only to demand better of our own systems but also to defend our values and institutions. When we have a say, we should speak. When we can cast a meaningful vote, we must. Untended, our freedoms wither. Rights are nothing unless they are exercised.

Fragile Democracies

The brisk deterioration of freedoms in Hong Kong has happened in the context not only of an increasingly totalitarian, confident and belligerent China, but also of a global surge in authoritarianism: 2020 was the first year since 2001 when there were more autocratic states in the world than democratic ones.[*] It is a trend that has quickened during the COVID-19 pandemic.[†] And for the first time since the Second World War, we are confronting a state with the power to ignore international action, and which in its language and actions is demonstrating a willingness to impose its hegemony through violence.[‡] It is increasingly well documented that the CCP is perpetrating a systematic act of mass genocide against the Uyghur minority. Yet today, public attention and the will to confront these atrocities seems lacking. In the end, the real victims of growing authoritarianism are not politicians denied office or a people denied representation, but those who are persecuted or disappeared for simply wishing to live without fear.

For me, the threat of authoritarianism, and in particular authoritarian or even totalitarian China, is a global emergency

---

[*] Varieties of Democracy report, 2020

[†] Freedom in the World 2021 report, Freedom House

[‡] 'China is building a sprawling network of missile silos, satellite imagery appears to show', https://edition.cnn.com/2021/07/02/asia/china-missile-silos-intl-hnk-ml/index.html; see also 'CCP 100: Xi warns China will not be "oppressed" in anniversary speech', https://www.bbc.co.uk/news/world-asia-china-57648236

every bit as pressing as the climate emergency. Both are existential threats. Climate change threatens life, while
authoritarianism threatens to strip life of its dignity. To live as
slaves to a political party, and in ignorance or fear, is not a life
worth living. Having silenced its own people, the CCP now
seeks to silence critical voices globally. China provides material support to and seeks to provide moral legitimacy for
oppressive regimes everywhere, and is a principal backer of
leaders in North Korea, Syria and Iran. More worryingly, this
support extends to failing and fragile democracies, from
Hungary and Turkey to Pakistan and Venezuela. China is
exporting a model of authoritarianism that it claims is superior to liberal democracy. In making the world safe for the
CCP, it is reshaping the globe.

Yet too many people continue to be blissfully ignorant of
what is happening beyond their own national politics, or see
this as a distant political issue rather than one that now
threatens their rights, freedoms and values. Too many people
in the international community don't seem to sense the mag-
nitude of the challenge we face, nor the urgency to address it.
Too many reduce the debate to a choice between the geopo-
litical hegemony of the US or China. Looked at this way, it is
reasonable to say we reject both. But the fact is that our freedoms define who we are and the lives we live. It is not about
geopolitics or choosing between competing superpowers – it
is about standing up for those values on which our dignity
depends.

In Western schools, students are taught the importance of
caring for the environment, and what they can do to make a
difference. We are taught about micro-aggressions and to be

sensitive to issues of culture and race. These are undoubtedly good things to do. But we must not lose sight of injustices that are occurring out of sight. There is painful irony in the fact that many of those who toppled statues of former slave owners are themselves clothed in the produce of forced labourers in Xinjiang.

The threat to our freedom has become, for me, the crisis of our era. Our reluctance to face up to it has to change. Our freedoms, human rights and liberal values need to be defended, as do open society and democracy. This starts with us being clear about what type of world we want to live in. We should follow up by formulating goals, setting agendas and taking action. Injustice and oppression are global, and our actions to address them must not end at our own borders. Democratic countries must work together to confront those that threaten our freedoms – and especially China, which is too large, too influential and too strong to deal with one on one. The free world needs an agreed strategy to defend itself and avoid being divided and then conquered.

Climate change was once viewed as a fringe political issue. Today the data supporting what was then considered fear-mongering is widely accepted, and in government, across boardrooms and in many homes, action is being taken to confront the challenge we face. We are prepared to change our businesses, the way we shop and the way we live our lives in order to do so, and we find strength and inspiration in doing what is right. Indeed, engagement with China, the world's largest polluter, is being driven because we realize that this must be a global effort – we understand that no matter how clean our own economies become, if we do not work to address the worst polluters our environment will continue to degrade. The same logic applies to the expansion of authoritarianism, which is polluting the world's politics.

Beyond Economic Coercion

China is a unique problem. No previous authoritarian power has combined its military and economic might, while integrating itself so thoroughly into our own economic and political systems. It has the second-largest economy in the world, and it could soon become the largest. It is now the EU's biggest trading partner, having overtaken the US in 2020.[*] Even with the Sino–US trade war, China remains the US's second-largest trading partner.[†] For the CCP these economic relationships are strategic, and a means by which not only to grow rich but also to promote its own agenda, demand subservience and acquire control.

China has consistently leveraged these economic relationships to acquire influence and to silence criticism. An early indicator was the way China reacted in 2010 to the decision to award the Nobel Peace Prize to the incarcerated Chinese literary critic and political essayist Liu Xiaobo, whom I quoted earlier. After the announcement China behaved belligerently, declaring relations with Norway were damaged. According

---

[*] 'China overtakes US as EU's biggest trading partner', https://www.bbc.co.uk/news/business-56093378

[†] 'Top Trading Partners - June 2021', https://www.census.gov/foreign-trade/statistics/highlights/toppartners.html

to the Chinese Foreign Ministry, 'The Nobel Committee giving the peace prize to such a person runs completely contrary to the aims of the prize.' At the prize ceremony, an empty chair symbolized the fact that Liu was detained and unable to attend. His family was barred from travel. It was the first time since 1935 that no relative or representative of the prize's recipient was present.* (Liu later died while under house arrest.)

The Chinese government responded by freezing political and economic relations with Norway, including implementing a range of sanctions against imports of Norwegian produce, most notably salmon. Diplomatic channels were closed or severely curtailed. For Beijing, as Hongkongers discovered, dialogue is not a means to address concerns but a reward for agreeing to Beijing's position.

It is worth remembering that the decision to award the Nobel Prize to Liu was not taken by the Norwegian government. The separation of powers between political and independent bodies is a hallmark of free societies as it underpins accountability. Beijing either does not know this – which seems unlikely, as it insists that it understands us, while we routinely misunderstand it – or simply expects other governments to operate in its own authoritarian manner. As Norway does not, it was punished.

Between 2011 and 2013, Chinese sanctions reduced direct exports of fish from Norway to China by between $125 and

---

* 'Norway and China Restore Ties, 6 Years After Nobel Prize Dispute', https://www.nytimes.com/2016/12/19/world/europe/china-norway-nobel-liu-xiaobo.html

176 million, with estimates of the fall in direct total exports ranging from $780 million to 1.3 billion. It was not until 2014 that trade levels again began to approach what they had been. This followed a flurry of compromising signals from the Norwegian government, which distanced itself from the Nobel Committee and took a more subdued position on human rights. Despite this, diplomatic and political relations between the two countries were not normalized for another two years. It would seem that China's coercion had worked.*

Since then, China has taken the same approach with a number of other democracies. Each time, the price demanded is not a compromise of their interests as much as their values. The Norwegian government's retreat from speaking up on human rights, not only in China but globally, was not representative of the values or the wishes of Norwegians. It undermined democracy – not in China, but in Norway. This is about protecting our freedoms and human rights on our own soil, defending independent institutions and the rights of our people to express their opinions. The economic becomes entangled with the political – because this is how it is in China.

Beijing's anger was stoked by the UK's decision not to allow the Chinese telecoms company Huawei to supply critical infrastructure, the decision of the broadcasting regulator Ofcom to ban the Chinese State broadcaster CGTN from

---

* 'Too big to fault? Effects of the 2010 Nobel Peace Prize on Norwegian exports to China and foreign policy', https://www.cmi.no/publications/ 5805-too-big-to-fault

broadcasting in the UK because of BBC reporting on the situation in Xinjiang, and because of the Home Office's British National Overseas (BNO) visa scheme to allow British nationals who, for reasons of history, are without the right of residency in the UK, to obtain this right. Beijing has also demanded that UK citizens and political figures refrain from criticizing China. On each of these issues Beijing is effectively demanding that the UK cede the rights of its own people in favour of its own interests – again, not in China, but in the UK. The UK government is in no position to dictate editorial decisions taken by the BBC, let alone the reporting of a journalist, nor to sway what decisions are made by Ofcom. Indeed, the value of those institutions to society depends on their independence from government. Whether or not to allow a company like Huawei, which was always categorized as a high-risk vendor, to bid to build the UK's critical infrastructure is a decision of state security. No country would allow foreign companies, especially those that are legally obliged to work with the security apparatus of a foreign and increasingly belligerent government, to be involved with their critical infrastructure if there were other choices available. China certainly does not. And yet it hypocritically demands that its companies must automatically have this right.

According to China, the UK's decision to open a pathway towards residency and citizenship for BNOs is an unacceptable interference in its internal affairs. Bear in mind that in the recent policies, the UK has not granted Hong Kong people British nationality. It has only allowed those who are already British nationals, or those who qualify for this status as former colonial subjects, a means to become full British nationals with residency rights in the UK.

It is sometimes said that China is responding to Western, or more specifically American, 'aggression'. Under President Biden, relations between the two mega-countries have only deteriorated further. Yet what exactly has the US done to so upset Beijing? The US has demanded that Beijing adhere to World Trade Organization rules, as all its members must, and to respect the norms of international diplomacy. It has expressed its concern over what China is doing to its own people, and termed what is happening in Xinjiang genocide. It has called out Chinese espionage, disinformation and illicit cyber activity in the US and stood in solidarity with other countries that have faced the same. President Obama, not usually thought of as the incarnation of American hubris and imperialism, initiated the American 'pivot to Asia' that China sees as containment. But it was Chinese assertiveness in the South China Sea that precipitated this pivot. China promised Obama that it was not building islands; then, when it started doing so, it promised they would not be militarized. China now operates several military bases in the contested waters. Is it really China reacting to Western aggression, or vice versa?

If America is the great enemy, it is Australia, the 'gum stuck on China's shoe',* that has felt the full force of Beijing's economic coercion. In 2020, as the world was gripped by a pandemic that left millions dead and ruined economies,

---

* 'Australia called "gum stuck to China's shoe" by state media in coronavirus investigation stoush', https://www.theguardian.com/world/2020/apr/28/australia-called-gum-stuck-to-chinas-shoe-by-state-media-in-coronavirus-investigation-stoush

Canberra called for an international inquiry into the origins of the coronavirus that was its cause. This was a perfectly reasonable suggestion. While it was believed that the coronavirus had begun in the Chinese city of Wuhan, where it was first detected, the proposal was not actually directed at China. Knowing where and how it had originated, whether in China or elsewhere, would help global leaders to understand the course of the pandemic and be better prepared in future. Despite the World Health Assembly (WHA) voting in favour of the inquiry, China ignored international opinion to single out Australia. According to China's Embassy in Canberra, Australia's assertion that the WHA vote had vindicated its request was 'nothing but a joke'.*

The Chinese government responded with numerous import bans, including on Australian wine, barley, coal, lobster, timber, red meat and cotton. Chinese students and tourists were warned against travel to the country, citing alleged racism. On campuses across Australia, where Chinese represent 39 per cent of international students, those who spoke out were harassed and threatened. Australian nationals whose relatives had disappeared in Xinjiang, and who chose to exercise their right to protest, received ominous phone calls. 'A couple of years ago, a lot of us were receiving phone calls at least once a day,' one such activist told the BBC. 'If we didn't pick up, there would be a voice message left in Chinese that would tell us we needed to renew our visas. I was born in Australia, my parents are Australian citizens and

---

* 'Australia and China spat over coronavirus inquiry deepens', https://www.reuters.com/article/us-health-coronavirus-australia-idUSKBN22V083

most of the community are Australian citizens. It's things like
that that shake the community.'*

The Chinese state co-ordinates, supports and is often directly involved in these efforts. Australia also became the
target of state-based cyberattacks, which increased in fre-
quency following Canberra's announcement.† The private
data of Australian citizens and parliamentarians were
exposed. Diplomatically, Australia was placed in deep freeze,
with Beijing cutting all communication with Australian min-
isters. China, simply put, does not play by the accepted
norms – what it seeks is total subservience.

As Beijing's diplomats pushed the line that it was the US
that was forcing states to take sides, Australian prime minister Scott Morrison's statement that Australia would not be
forced into 'binary choices' between China and the US was
greeted in Beijing with the words that Australia had to 'face
up to the problems, correct mistakes and create conditions
for bringing bilateral relations back on track'.‡

The mistakes that Beijing expected Australia to 'correct'
were made clear when in November 2020 it presented Canberra with a list of fourteen sins.§ These included passing

---

* 'The students calling out China on Australia's campuses', https://www.bbc
   .co.uk/news/world-australia-56478621

† 'Australia sees China as main suspect in state-based cyberattacks, sources
   say', https://www.reuters.com/article/us-australia-cyber-idUSKBN23P3T5

‡ 'China demands that Australia fixes "mistakes" to repair relationship',
   https://www.theaustralian.com.au/news/latest-news/china-demands-that-
   australia-fixes-mistakes-to-repair-relationship/news-story/952b17f0986
   fef7542e71ee06f32ca43

§ 'China shows official list of reasons for anger with Australia', https://
   www.9news.com.au/national/china-australia-tensions-beijing-
   government-grievance-list-with-canberra/adc10554-e4e9-4a19-970e-
   81949501a1ad

Foreign Interference Laws and a new Foreign Relations Law to protect the country from malign foreign infiltration; the decision to exclude Huawei from its critical infrastructure; speaking out on human rights and on the South China Sea; and siding with a US-led 'anti-China campaign' in calling for an inquiry into the origins of COVID-19. All these actions had been taken to protect Australia and address human rights violations. One of Australia's many other sins, in China's eyes, was to allow a critical discourse on what was happening in Hong Kong. Beijing was now effectively demanding that the Australian government deny freedom of expression and silence the press, academia, parliamentarians and the public, as the CCP does in China. To expect this, and to punish Australia economically and diplomatically for not being more authoritarian, China presents as non-interference and respect.

Despite Beijing's economic coercion, China remains Australia's largest trading partner. Headlines about plummeting trade masked the fact that overall trade between the two nations is down just 2 per cent in value since China's import bans.* New markets were found for many Australian products: for example, much of the wine once destined for China was sold in the UK. Australian exports, which Chinese authorities had kept at sea for over a year, having refused to allow ships to either dock in or leave Chinese waters – effectively

---

* 'Most Australian trade with China has plummeted 40 per cent amid tensions, DFAT reveals', https://www.abc.net.au/news/2021-03-25/australian-trade-with-china-plummets/100029910

holding their crews captive* – began to find other ways of reaching their markets. Seafood, which has a short shelf life, still made its way on to Chinese tables through Hong Kong.† For all the bluster, China was also careful not to limit the importation of Australian commodities it could not easily source from elsewhere.

This bullying and hypocrisy on the world stage are a taste of the future China is working towards. Thankfully, Australia is strong enough, and free enough, to ride out Chinese attempts at coercion. While some Australian businesses have suffered as a result, it is a small price to pay for Australian sovereignty and in defence of its values as a free, open and tolerant society. Australians, once bullish about the 'China dream', have learnt to understand the true nature of the Chinese state under President Xi. So have Norwegians, and an increasing number of countries around the world. Sweden has been threatened,‡ EU think tanks and lawmakers sanctioned,§ and Belgium targeted by cyberattacks.⁋ Public

---

* 'Sailors Stranded for Months as China Refuses to Let Ships Unload Australian Coal', https://www.nytimes.com/2020/12/26/business/coal-ships-china-australia.html

† 'Banned Australian lobsters are sneaking into China via Hong Kong', https://www.bloomberg.com/news/articles/2021-06-24/banned-australian-lobsters-are-sneaking-into-china-via-hong-kong

‡ 'China Tries to Put Sweden on Ice', https://thediplomat.com/2019/12/china-tries-to-put-sweden-on-ice

§ 'EU-China: Sanctions, threats and boycotts see relations enter downward spiral', https://www.euronews.com/2021/03/31/eu-china-sanctions-threats-and-boycotts-see-relations-enter-downward-spiral

⁋ 'Revealed: Government ministry hacked by foreign power', https://www.brusselstimes.com/news/belgium-all-news/170919/revealed-government-ministry-hacked-by-foreign-power-china-2019-information-national-crisis-hafnium-affair-microsoft-exchange

opinion may be turning, but this has not yet meaningfully translated into the will to act.

International brands have also been targeted. In March 2021, the Chinese government launched a campaign to boycott those that had joined the Better Cotton Initiative, an international multi-stakeholder group that promotes better standards in cotton farming, expressing concerns over the use of forced labour in Xinjiang. Participating companies including H&M, Nike, Uniqlo and Adidas subsequently put the China market before their concern for human rights and the concerns of their domestic customers and withdrew their support. Others, including Hugo Boss, Asics and Muji, went so far as to advertise that they would be using Xinjiang cotton. Nevertheless, Chinese online stores removed products, physical stores were delisted from the Chinese Web and a wave of videos of patriotic fans burning their products were promoted and went viral in Chinese heavily state-controlled social media. Many brands are yet to understand that there is no middle way between supporting basic human rights and appeasing China.

According to Beijing, of course, there are no human rights abuses happening in Xinjiang. It accused the Western media of smearing China and of inciting subversion against the CCP. To Beijing, companies that do not willingly promote its false narrative should not make money in China. When the Arsenal footballer Mesut Özil quite understandably expressed his concern about what is happening to the Turkic Uyghur people of Xinjiang, China stopped broadcasting Arsenal football matches until the club silenced its player and distanced itself from his comments. Özil soon found himself out of favour at the club.[*] Such pressure to censor sports, celebrities and other public figures is now routine. Brands and public figures who speak out on China, where serious human rights abuses are systemic, are presented by the Chinese government as part of a racist conspiracy against China.[†]

Even though the effectiveness of China's economic coercion varies, and is often not as damaging as it wants us to believe, the level of belligerence shown by the Chinese state and the tone it takes is consistent. It is hostile and insulting. Should we continue to accept this behaviour and an unbalanced relationship with China, as we have done for too long, we only encourage this behaviour. The China we face today is in part a product of our complacency. The CCP has fed off our goodwill and trust. Authoritarian regimes do not build trusting societies – unelected and unaccountable, they rely on distraction and suppression.

When we can no longer expect to be able to speak up for our values, to call out injustices and be critical of grave abuses of human rights, our own freedoms are eroded and our democracy is weakened. Fragile democracies like Hungary and Turkey have already gone this way – even the great liberal project that is Europe could not stop it from happening. Indeed, now Hungary vetoes European Union action against China, including against Hong Kong. Authoritarianism expands and

---

* 'Craven Arsenal abandon Mesut Özil over his stance on China's Uighur persecution', https://www.theguardian.com/football/2019/dec/16/arsenal-mesut-ozil-uighurs-china

† '#StopAsianHate: Chinese diaspora targeted by CCP disinformation campaign', https://www.aspistrategist.org.au/stopasianhate-chinese-diaspora-targeted-by-ccp-disinformation-campaign

the free world shrinks as our capacity to see China for what it is and to stand up for our values diminishes. Through investment and economic ties, vaccine diplomacy and in such ambitious projects as the Belt and Road Initiative, Beijing is seeking to change our lives. It will do this by picking us off one by one, just as it has done to the people of Hong Kong.

The democratic world needs to unite behind a vision of a global future. It is time for free people and free nations to stand together against this systemic threat to our way of life. We must understand that this is not about any kind of racist or discriminatory policies, not about China-bashing or scapegoating, not about launching another war or colour revolution, but about defending our own free and open societies. We must realize that speaking truth to the people of China, many of whom have no choice but to live in a false narrative dictated by the CCP, is the only way Chinese people will know what is being done in their name. If we allow the CCP to continue to take advantage of our openness and freedoms to seed its own reality in our societies, to sow divisions among our peoples and between states, and to feed our greed at the expense of our conscience, the CCP will rise and the decline in our democracy will reach a point of no return.

Confronting Global Authoritarianism

For me, taking this stand is personal. Hong Kong was once Asia's most vibrant, open and free city, and a model for now democratic Taiwan. In a few short years, I have watched it wither into the quasi-authoritarian police state that it is today. The story I have told in this book should serve as a warning to the free world.

I am fortunate to have met other human rights and democracy activists from around the world, some from places where the situation in their home countries is worse than it is in Hong Kong. We all feel a deep connection with our homelands and with our people. A sense of loss affects us deeply. But what for me distinguishes the activist from the pretender is that, despite having more reason than most to hate, that is not what drives them. I do not hate China, nor do I hate institutions. Rather, I oppose institutionalized injustice and political persecution. You fight the lie, and hope that the liar will admit to his lie and begin telling the truth. Whether we are confronting oppression in Syria, North Korea, Iran, Russia, Belarus, Venezuela or in China and Hong Kong, we are ultimately part of the same fight for human dignity. Our stories may differ, but the threat we face, though varying in degree, is the same. Those who are truly fighting for anything worth fighting for are driven not by politics but by values.

Together we must hold dictators accountable. We must call out lies and disinformation. We must not be bought or cajoled into silence. We need not respond with hate. But we must speak up, and we must act.

We have seen the trajectory of China's astonishing economic growth, and with it China's growing arrogance. Those who had hoped for a better China, and that engagement would lead to a more accommodating regime, need to accept that they got it wrong. We need to accept that China is heading towards being, if it is not already, a hyper-nationalist totalitarian state. We can no longer be blind to its Cold War rhetoric, its military build-up, nor its manipulation of international institutions. We can no longer ignore that it is at war with our own domestic institutions, from independent courts to the free press, and seeks to control the discourse by silencing all critics.

In the conduct of our businesses and investments we must decide what is important to us, and send a clear message to those businesses that do not value our freedoms to decide what type of society they wish to operate in. People already take to the streets to protest against businesses using fur, and our universities cut ties with companies seen as not doing enough for climate change; and yet we readily open accounts with British banks like HSBC and Standard Chartered that openly support Hong Kong's National Security Law, even though the UK government has declared it to be a serious breach of international law – one that is being used to politically persecute British nationals. We need to ask such companies what they value and whom they serve.

We have to defend our people and our society from disinformation. We must be as sensitive to Chinese and Russian disinformation as we are when censoring extremism from within our own societies. We should not only tell the truth, but also be robust in refuting lies. We need to match reports on what is happening in Xinjiang and on what happened in Hong Kong with equally important explainers refuting the conspiracies and lies promoted by Beijing. The BBC and the *Telegraph* may initially have taken Beijing at its word when it claimed that there were no human rights abuses in

Xinjiang, but what is important is that they then followed up by reporting that these promises were empty.* We have to know not only what is happening, but how we are being lied to.

We need to be aware that authoritarian states, principally Russia and China, are seeking to manipulate us through social media, and that while social media companies are responding, the fluidity of this type of influence operation makes it hard to prevent. We should know that networks of bots were set up by the Chinese to shift the narrative on Hong Kong, and that these networks are now being used by China to promote alternative narratives on Xinjiang and to deepen divisions in the West over issues of social justice. We must spread awareness, too, that the Chinese state is actively recruiting social media influencers.† While it goes against the values of a free society to censor such messages, open debate presupposes good faith, and they should be exposed for what they are.

International organizations are in need of reform and

---

* 'Xinjiang 2.0: Is China's persecution of millions of Muslim Uyghurs entering a sinister new phase?', https://www.telegraph.co.uk/news/2021/06/13/ xinjiang-20-chinas-persecution-millions-muslim-uyghurs-entering; see also 'China's pressure and propaganda – the reality of reporting Xinjiang', https://www.bbc.co.uk/news/world-asia-china-55666153

† 'China state TV channel CGTN enlists UK student influencers', https:// www.thetimes.co.uk/article/china-state-tv-channel-cgtn-enlists-uk- student-influencers-dw9v5sbnc; 'Beijing funds British YouTubers to further its propaganda war', https://www.thetimes.co.uk/article/beijing- funds-british-youtubers-to-further-its-propaganda-war-x5gqp5fg0; 'How China Built a Twitter Propaganda Machine Then Let It Loose on Coronavirus', https://www.propublica.org/article/how-china-built-a- twitter-propaganda-machine-then-let-it-loose-on-coronavirus

reinforcement. We should embrace universal values and build our institutions around them. We need to move on from the idea of tackling human rights violations on an individual or case-by-case basis. We must wake up to the very clear patterns that are emerging. We should finally move on from our past, and see intervention on the grounds of human rights not as an act of aggression or imperialism but as a moral action in defence of victims. We must distinguish between true sovereignty and the misleading language of 'sovereignty' and 'internal affairs' which authoritarian governments use as a means to evade supervision and to get away with crimes against humanity.

We must have our own red lines. A rules-based order that is easily manipulated to allow the very abuses such rules are meant to prevent is not fit for purpose, and only provides a veneer of credibility to oppressive states. The United Nations Human Rights Council should not be composed of a majority of countries who reject human rights, or subscribe to a very restrictive and politically driven definition of what they are – yet this is today the case. Likewise, the European Union cannot be allowed to be held ransom by one country, especially one that no longer meets or respects the Union's ideals and standards in governance.

Change will not be easy. It begins with affirming what we believe. We need to stop being complacent, realize the threat we face and learn again to appreciate that our freedoms cannot be taken for granted. We must rediscover faith in our system, and while seeking to hold our own institutions accountable, our criticisms need context and perspective. We should stand together with other democratic and free states as a coalition of shared values and ideals. Each member of this community will be different, and the freedoms we enjoy will vary to some degree, but we will be united by the type of world we would like to see. Diplomacy has to evolve, as it did at the end of the Cold War. We must no longer be so naive about the way in which oppressive regimes use the language of our values but act in the opposite way – China, remember, claims to be the most successful democracy in the world. We should unite around a shared respect for open societies and liberal institutions, the rule of law, a free press and the fundamental freedoms: of thought, conscience, expression and information.

Communities have a role to play. The twinning of our towns and cities could be an opportunity to reaffirm our values; as a community or organization we can be more selective about whom we engage with, and how. When we interact with Russia or China, should we see those beholden to Putin and Xi as representing all Russian and Chinese people? Might we not also associate with those who dare wish to see their country free? The days when engagement with China means tacitly agreeing to deplatform dissidents and to marginalize or silence our own critical voices must end.

The influence of authoritarian tyranny respects no borders. It is a mindset. We need to see each falling domino as part of a wider trend. Thus, the military coup in Myanmar in February 2021 should not be regarded or dealt with in isolation, nor should the violent suppression – aided by the Russian government – of pro-democracy protestors in Belarus. Both are achievements for the authoritarian camp and have wider international repercussions. Our past failure to mark clear red lines has only empowered such regimes to act in ways that a more robust approach would have stopped. We let China get away lightly with what it did in Tibet, and within China proper, in the name of building a 'harmonious society' – the result has been Hong Kong and Xinjiang.

Authoritarian regimes can appear in different guises. China claims to be socialist, yet provides relatively little welfare support to its people and has emasculated trade unions. It stokes nationalist fervour and presents itself as championing Chinese civilization, and yet rather than embrace the diversity of the true Chinese identity and experience, it is brutally moulding a new image that places the CCP regime as central to what it means to be Chinese. Political ideology is only ever there to justify dictatorial and oppressive forms of governance. What they are is authoritarian, and what unites all authoritarian regimes is a fear of their own people. This is why authoritarian states devote significant resources to propaganda promoting the 'superiority' of their model of government and seeking to undermine our confidence in our own systems. Knowing they have no popular legitimacy, they seek to undermine credibility in democracies everywhere. In rejecting China's assertion of 'better governance under a one-party regime', not only must democratic governments themselves start to work better, but we also need to see democratic accountability operating properly in the interest of a free and fair world at the international level.

A coalition of the free is not just about confronting state-based and systemic threats. Addressing global issues, whether climate change, poverty, development or future health emergencies, will be easier if international norms are set by states that respect them because they are not solely focused on regime survival. As COVID-19 showed, even on an issue of global public health, which should not have been one of particular political sensitivity to the CCP, the instinct was to cover up, deny and to blame failures on 'foreign forces'. Can we trust a country that allows politics to dictate its official figures, including GDP, to be honest about carbon emissions? Equally, it is simply better to work on tackling poverty with a democratically accountable government that is not creaking under the weight of its own corruption. It's easier to do business with a government that has a popular mandate, in a system designed to allow for smooth changes of administration.

A more democratic international community is not going to come about through unilateral action, and neither should it. Every country that values its freedom should take a step towards making this happen. Without co-ordination between like-minded democracies, China is of a size to be able to target individual states and to shift them into its own orbit. Should others go the way of Hong Kong, the facade of freedom will be all that the CCP will tolerate. China will seek to make an example of them, to cow others into accepting what it presents as its unstoppable rise to global ascendancy.

We have a moral responsibility to stand shoulder to shoulder with our allies and friends, and to see an assault on them as an assault on us all. We must not shy away from strong, targeted collective action. We should not mistake opposition to the CCP regime as anti-China, nor conflate the Party with the people. We ought to be honest and constructively critical of China. At the same time, we should not allow China to dictate the terms of engagement and dialogue. In short, on the world stage, we should treat China as we treat any other country.

Conscience, Activism and 'Be Water'

My life could so easily have been different. I remember vividly that I struggled to decide whether I should apply to run the student union in 2014. In Lingnan University, we had to apply jointly as a committee. Applications need a group of at least eleven, and I had failed to recruit enough students. Alongside four others, I had been campaigning for half a year to find the right people. I had organized meetings, distributed leaflets and knocked on doors. Yet all these efforts were in vain; on the day before the deadline, I did not have enough people to form a cabinet with me. I sat in the student union office, frustrated, thinking I should probably just focus on my schoolwork and spend time doing things that made me happier.

As I was sitting on the sofa, a former student leader approached me to tell me about another post on the council. The branch that held the executive accountable was falling vacant because no one was running. I hesitated. If I were to run on my own, I would have a lonely and probably thankless year ahead of me. I felt exhausted and lost. I thought that perhaps I should demur and find other ways to be involved. Nonetheless, someone had to hold power accountable. After going back and forth in my mind, I agreed to run.

If I were put in the same situation again, with the same

mental state, I could easily see myself declining. It felt pretty insignificant, but I can see now that this single choice changed my life for ever. Following your conscience is often about making a seemingly small decision not to be selfish with your time, or refusing to look the other way. I was only in my first year of university, but already I had a feeling that society needed students who would speak up when they saw injustice and who dared to demand change. I resolved to make the choice I could be proud of. The unintended consequences were gigantic, but I have never regretted my decision.

Many people are placed in much more complicated and difficult situations – a police officer being asked to take a bribe, a forensic doctor being asked to lie about the cause of death, a soldier being asked to shoot protestors on the street. If each of us can act with conscience, that collective moral power alone can defend justice. Sometimes it isn't easy to discern the outcome of your choice. But at the end, when you look back, I can promise that you will remember the feeling in your heart when you made the decision.

Politics and activism may seem distant from our everyday lives. I believe that acting with conscience is already political, and many of us are doing our part without knowing it. When you follow your conscience, you are only ever one step away from activism.

Activism takes many forms, depending on the history, culture and values of the community. In an undemocratic and highly unequal society like Hong Kong, much of it, whether for workers' rights, social justice or for greater equality, happened under the umbrella of the pro-democracy movement. When the system provides neither democratic representation nor accountability, addressing societal issues necessarily starts with a call for a political voice.

If activism is about pushing for social progress, then the actions taken and the changes activists wish to achieve can vary widely. What binds our varied efforts is how we see ourselves. To become an activist is to transform your life – to consciously devote a greater part of yourself to a collective pursuit; to sublimate your individual interests and personal goals to be part of a movement. Activism is a way of life.

Most of us have at some period sought to find meaning in our lives. Many of us grow up being taught to be good, hardworking citizens – to get a good education and job, to take care of family and friends, to behave responsibly and to show charity to others. In Hong Kong, the path we are meant to take in life is laid out for us by society – we are raised with clear expectations. We are rarely challenged to think about the meaning of that path, yet many of us still have the question at the back of our minds. Being an activist has been my journey to answering these questions. It has required waking up to the injustices around me, and realizing the role of my own agency in making change.

At each stage along my journey, I have simply done what I felt to be right by the people I know. I realize that I cannot represent everyone, and that there are many who believe I do not represent them at all. But my life in Hong Kong and in China before that taught me that people are not always free to say what is in their heart. I have also learnt that freedom is felt differently by different people. Some people will internalize their fears so deeply that they are no longer conscious of them, and yet fear still manifests in their actions and reasoning. The people I represent, and the people I believe are in most need of representation, are those whose fears are denied.

Life as an activist is a tortured existence. I am grateful to be doing what is most meaningful to me – what I feel, in a way, compelled to do. And yet it is very unstable and difficult. There is no surety in this life, nor security; it is racked with self-doubt, as each decision I make is taken with so many people in mind. It is exhausting.

I sometimes wonder what might have happened if my life had panned out differently. Perhaps if I had been born into a society where there was not an acute crisis, I might have led quite a normal existence. I used to hope for an exciting and prosperous career, and the opportunity to elevate my family into a better, more comfortable, lifestyle. It once meant every-thing to me to see my mother happy in the knowledge that her son was doing fine. Too many people around me did not make the grade, and life led them down very dark roads. At least my family didn't have to see me take that route. How-ever, the path I have taken has also caused them great heartache. Family has always meant a lot to me, and now I am separated from them.

I have made my mother furious at times. She wept when I was first arrested in 2014, and could not sleep while I was held in detention. She was always tired when she visited me in jail. It took her hours on public transport to get to the prison, and her legs always hurt after she had walked up the ramp to the prison block. Once, she cut her finger while working as a cleaner, because she'd had so little sleep worrying about her son. In a way, this was all because of me.

It was as if everything I had done was going against the son I was meant to be, and had been raised to believe I was. I was meant to provide a better life for her and the family. It often left me feeling indebted to my mother, who had lived her life so that mine might be better. And yet I have never once felt that I have done wrong. In fact, I feel – despite being raised to keep my head down and not cause trouble – that what I was doing was 'right'. It was right not by me, nor by my family, but by our community and by my home.

I found meaning in life not by living the way my family wished, but by taking the decisions that align with my values. In a society like Hong Kong, among the community I was raised in, this is a radical departure from the norm. Yet I was far from alone. In 2014, when a generation of Hong-kongers rose in protest, it was not only about democracy and our identity: I sense also a rejection of society's lie that their lives must be defined by others.

I have found true meaning in the dignity of a people who are free to embrace their values. This is the Hong Kong spirit that gave my home its energy. Hong Kong was defined not by what office clerks did as they sat behind their desks, but the conversations they had when they met in the street. It was in raucous newspapers like *Apple Daily* that Hong Kong dared to be different. Those were my people, and that was my community.

Life is full of dilemmas, and most of the time there are no perfect choices. It is about give and take. What we take and what we give is guided by our values. From the moment I first considered myself an activist, somehow, all that mattered to me were the people. For them, I was willing to give up everything.

'Empty your mind. Be formless, shapeless – like water. You put water into a cup, it becomes the cup. You put water into a bottle, it becomes the bottle. You put it in a teapot, it becomes the teapot. Now water can flow or it can crash. Be water, my friend.' So said one of Hong Kong's most famous sons, the martial artist Bruce Lee. 'Be Water' has become one of the central slogans, and ideas, of the Hong Kong protest movement.

Confronted by the most powerful, controlling and repressive authoritarian power, protestors must be like water. We must be able to flow over any obstacle and take on any form. Before we can shape our home and our circumstance, we must be able to survive in circumstances created by those who wish to suppress our voices. Activists must be adaptable and remain true to their values and beliefs, as it is in this that we find solidarity with others. No matter how grim the situation may seem, nor how weak we may at times feel, we must not forget how quickly things can change – how in even shallow waters waves can quickly form. We must not forget the power of water.

Being an Activist

In the early summer of 2020, it was clear that a major crackdown was coming. I knew that if I stayed in Hong Kong I faced being jailed by Beijing, and I wasn't sure whether the authorities might prevent me from boarding a flight; but I knew that leaving was now the only realistic way to continue my international advocacy work.

When I arrived at the airport, I was so nervous. I handed over my passport for checking, and they let me through. I boarded the plane and sat with my seat belt buckled as the pre-flight checks were performed. Then we took off, and I knew I was safe.

I was sitting in the window seat, and I looked down at Hong Kong. By night it was the most gorgeous cityscape in the world. At that moment, I understood it was probably the last time I would see the city that I've been fighting for, that I served, that I was jailed for. Probably the last time I would see the skyline, perhaps the last time I would see many of the people I loved.

It is not easy being an activist. For me, a good activist is characterized by commitment, self-discipline and a sense of calm. Without commitment, nothing can be achieved. Social movements are always a struggle, as you are up against the powerful, whether governments or large corporations. By definition, political might and the power of capital generate huge advantages. Activists only have the power of people. There will inevitably be defeats, and times when the situation may seem hopeless. But we must persevere. Only with commitment and determination is change possible.

As an activist, you have to remember that one day you could be someone whom others will look up to. You will need to set an example, and you will be scrutinized. There will be those who wish to find your weakness, to embarrass you, and to twist what you may once have said or written to hurt you and the movement. Your supporters will seek insight and inspiration from you, and you will be expected to help empower them. The agency others seek they will look for in you.

It is best to be cautious, and to be in control. Don't get carried away by your emotions. Accept that you will let some people down, that some will misrepresent you, and that others will always find fault. Even people within the movement may criticize or attack you – in any movement there will be politics. People will chastise you for whatever reason they can think of – your background, your appearance or your attitude. (The teenage activist Greta Thunberg, for example, has been repeatedly fat-shamed by Chinese state media.) Try not to take it personally. Hate is never constructive, nor does it help a movement deserving of respect.

Learn to identify and to welcome constructive criticism, including from your most ferocious critics. Never pass up an opportunity to learn. Life is a continual learning experience, and you shouldn't be afraid to admit mistakes or to change your view. As John Maynard Keynes once said, 'When the facts change, I change my mind – what do you do?' Everything evolves: people, circumstances and movements. What is most important is to be honest with yourself.

In adversity and defeat, find opportunities to learn and to grow stronger as a person. Learn lessons to be better prepared the next time. See each setback as a test of your commitment, each challenge as a test of character. Remain calm if you can, and if you feel you're losing control, try to seek out the time and space that will allow for perspective.

The truth is that an activist is not a hero. Neither is activism a hobby or a fad. Real activism is not fun. It is something you find yourself drawn to do because you feel deep down that it is important. Activism begins with values, and should be driven by them. You don't have to be especially clever, brave, principled or good to be an activist. You have to care enough about an issue to want to see change for the better.

No Action Is Meaningless

The 4 June candlelight vigil has a special meaning for me. It was the first protest I ever attended, and my first engagement with civil society. It commemorates an emotive event for many Hongkongers and Chinese people around the world – the 1989 Tiananmen Square Massacre. It matters not only because we remember those who died, but because so much has been done by the CCP to write it out of our history. It represents the conflict between truth and lies – and the inner hurt we are expected to carry, unacknowledged, in building Beijing's revisionist China.

In 2021, for the second year running, the vigil was banned. As in the year before, COVID-19 was cited as the official reason – and yet, as in the year before, the subsequent rhetoric from Beijing's mouthpieces in Hong Kong suggested the real issue was patriotism. Despite the ban in 2020, thousands still choose to risk arrest to gather in commemoration, as has always been the case. It is one of the largest annual protest events in the city. I was one of the attendants in 2020, and I was also one of the many to be charged by the police.

In 2021 the authorities took no chance. Although Hong Kong was almost unaffected by the virus, any sign of protest or remembrance had to be stopped. The police barricaded all entrances into Victoria Park, the traditional protest site.

Pro-Beijing figures were rolled out to announce that any act was likely to be a violation of the city's new National Security Law. It would not simply be a case of trespassing or unlawful assembly. This happened in the context of a severe crack-down on Hong Kong's freedoms and civil liberties. Education was being reformed. People were encouraged to report on each other for unpatriotic activities. China had begun a campaign against 'historic nihilism' – meaning any view of history that did not conform to the CCP line. People were erasing personal accounts and censoring their content online. 'Tank man', the iconic image of a man standing in the way of PLA tanks in Tiananmen in 1989, was inexplicably removed from the internet search engine Bing worldwide. Any mention of it has long been scrubbed away within China, but Chinese censorship now reached boldly across borders. In Hong Kong, remembrance was not only unpatriotic, it was illegal.

A few days before 4 June, netizens and campaigners began suggesting new ways to protest. They appealed to the public not to assemble at Victoria Park, but to light a candle wherever they happened to be. To hold a minute's silence at 8 p.m. was also suggested, as would usually happen at the vigil.

The authorities responded by threatening to arrest anyone caught conducting 'rituals', wearing black clothing or chanting protest slogans. The act of lighting a candle was deemed 'provocative' and a possible threat to national security.

All the same, on the evening of 4 June many people dressed in black travelled to Causeway Bay, where Victoria Park is, to wander around the district. Police conducted 'stop and search' on any persons they considered 'suspicious'. The young were especially targeted. The threat of a draconian and unjust law, coupled with arbitrary harassment, was intended to scare people from the streets. Yet hundreds of people came nevertheless.

People declared that they were merely 'shopping' or 'out for a jog'. Unable to light candles, many simply switched on the flashlight of their mobile phones. Hundreds of thousands of people across the city did so, turning parts of Hong Kong into a galaxy of stars.

Regimes will always try to stop us from exercising our right to protest. They will try to silence us with fear. They will try to co-opt us with promises. This is the nature of oppression – to deny us our freedom to think and act for ourselves. But no matter the circumstances, there are always means of protest, no matter how small. Even in the darkest times, we can resist cruelty by small acts of kindness. We can outsmart them. We can be flexible. We can be creative. As long as we keep thinking and challenging ourselves, there is always a way forward.

The day after 4 June, news outlets across the free world had a new story to tell: that of the creativity of Hong Kong people. The *New York Times* reported:

> *Democracy advocates in Hong Kong are grasping for new ways to sustain the memory of the Chinese military's bloody crackdown on the Tiananmen Square protests, under a government increasingly bent on repressing dissent and free expression.*[*]

---

* 'Subdued but Not Silenced, Hong Kong Tries to Remember Tiananmen Massacre', https://www.nytimes.com/2021/06/04/world/asia/china-tiananmen-massacre.html

The *Guardian* ran the headline, 'Hong Kong finds new ways to remember Tiananmen Square amid vigil ban' and reported how Hongkongers had turned to other ways of protesting, creating pieces of performance art and laying flowers at symbolic locations, to continue the movement.*

Beijing has tried so hard to erase the memory of 1989, but in doing so it has given the world another story. Denial has immortalized its memory among free people. Now we all need to stand firm to defend our freedoms, to ensure truth is not determined by dictators.

Today an emboldened CCP believes the future belongs to the People's Republic of China. It seeks a world that is safe for authoritarianism by eroding freedoms everywhere. It believes in the power of propaganda and lies engineered by technological advancement to shape the minds not only of Chinese citizens, but of all people. It seeks to define the global discourse and to set the rules. It is emboldened by our greed, and the craven and self-serving people who place the promise of material wealth over the rights and freedoms of all – the rights and freedoms upon which a free and vibrant society is founded. Hong Kong may not be the most oppressed city in the world, but it is especially important as the leading example of how a prosperous, free, open and vibrant society can be undermined. It is the canary in the coal mine for the free world.

Hong Kong people stood up to protest because they

---

* 'Hong Kong finds new ways to remember Tiananmen Square amid vigil ban', https://www.theguardian.com/world/2021/jun/04/hong-kong-finds-new-ways-to-remember-tiananmen-square-amid-vigil-ban

remembered what had been promised. They stood up because they remembered that all people are born free and as equals. As long as we remember this, and remember who we are, no one can deny us our freedom. 'The limits of tyrants are prescribed by the endurance of those whom they oppress,' wrote Frederick Douglass. Freedom triumphs as long as we remember to endure.

ABOUT THE AUTHORS

Nathan Law became Hong Kong's youngest-ever lawmaker in 2016 but was later deposed through the intervention of the Chinese Communist Party. He has since been nominated for a Nobel Peace Prize and was named as one of the people of 2020 in both *The Observer* and *TIME* magazine.

nathanlawkc.com | @nathanlawkc

Evan Fowler, a Hong Kong native, is an independent writer and researcher focusing on Hong Kong and China affairs.